in your pocket

MAIN CONTRIBUTOR: GEORGE MCDONALD

PHOTOGRAPH CREDITS
Photos supplied by The Travel Library:
title page, 97; Stuart Black front cover, back cover 7, 8, 12, 15, 17, 20, 27, 28, 30, 37, 39, 41, 45(t,b), 50, 51, 52, 53, 55, 57, 58, 59, 61, 67, 68, 69, 71, 72, 74, 76, 77, 78, 79, 85, 86(t,b), 87, 88, 89, 90(l,r), 93, 94, 99, 101, 103, 105, 106, 108, 109, 111, 113, 115, 121, 122; Freelance Pictures 44, 49, 60, 63, 81, 82, 125; John Lawrence 4, 25, 38, 65; R Richardson 36, 43, 92; E Zaplatine 31, 32, 33, 34, 40, 117.
Other Photos:
Musée des Beaux-Arts, France/Giraudon/Bridgeman Art Library 11; Tourism Flanders-Brussels 80.

Front cover: flower sellers in the Grand-Place;
back cover: pavement cafés in the Îlot Sacré district;
title page: Manneken Pis.

MANUFACTURE FRANÇAISE DES PNEUMATIQUES MICHELIN
Place des Carmes-Déchaux – 63000 Clermont-Ferrand (France)

Dépôt légal Jan 2000 – ISBN 2-06-651001-7 – ISSN 1272-1689

Printed in Spain 2-01/2

MICHELIN TRAVEL PUBLICATIONS
Hannay House
39 Clarendon Road
WATFORD Herts WD17 1JA - UK
☎ (01923) 205240
www.ViaMichelin.com

MICHELIN TRAVEL PUBLICATIONS
Michelin North America
One Parkway South
GREENVILLE, SC 29615
☎ 1-800 423-0485
www.ViaMichelin.com

CONTENTS

INTRODUCTION

Brussels used to be the capital of a modest country. Today it is Capital of Europe, riding the fast-track to global prominence and changing rapidly. Marble-and-glass palaces have sprung up to house the Euro-institutions. Multinational corporations, embassies, business associations, news organisations, lobbyists and consultants have piled in, all with an unerring instinct for the source of power and fountain of largesse that the European Union represents.

Yet an older Brussels has proved resistant

to change. Brand Whitlock, an early-20C American ambassador, captured its spirit thus: 'One must … loiter during long afternoons in the crowded, narrow, sloping streets of the lower town, lunch in the little restaurants in the neighbourhood of the Grand-Place … and somehow learn to know and appreciate the tang and flavour of the local accent, and, by slow degrees, find one's way into and be accepted by the great heart of the city that is not like any other in the world.'

Floodlighting at night brings a golden glow to the gilded façades of the noble guildhalls on Grand-Place.

Brussels isn't known as 'Burgundian Brussels' for nothing. The city has more Michelin Star restaurants per person than Paris and it's almost impossible to eat badly here. Throw in Belgium's 400 beers, each with its own special glass, 300 artisanal cheeses, and a host of regional cuisine specialities from Flanders and Wallonia, and the danger is you'll be too busy waving knives and forks around, and quenching your thirst, to appreciate other aspects of the city.

True, you'll find no museums with the overwhelming breadth of the Louvre and British Museum, but in the Musées Royaux des Beaux-Arts you'll see works by Bruegel, Rubens and Magritte, among many others, and on the plus side you can get round Brussels' smaller institutions more easily and take satisfaction in unhurried perusal. For a symbol of the city, take your pick between cheeky Manneken Pis and the awesome Atomium, and as a bonus save yourself a lot of airfares by touring Europe in miniature at Mini-Europe.

When you're ready to get beyond the city limits, the Flemish art towns of Mechelen and Leuven, and emblematic sights in Wallonia at Villers-la-Ville and Seneffe, are all within easy reach. You'll need more time than you have.

GEOGRAPHY

Brussels straddles Belgium's language and cultural boundary between Dutch-speaking Flanders and French-speaking Wallonia – a fault-line that on a wider scale mirrors western Europe's historic division between the Germanic north and Latin south. Antwerp and Holland lie to the north; Charleroi and France to the south; north-west are Ghent, Bruges and the Flemish coastal resorts; south-east the River Meuse, Liège and the rolling Ardennes hills.

The circular gallery running round the immense bronze dome of the Basilique du Sacré-Coeur, in Koekelberg, offers fine views right across the city.

The bilingual Belgian capital and its surroundings form Région de Bruxelles-Capitale (Brussels Capital Region), which with Flanders and Wallonia comprise the Belgian federal state. With 950 000 inhabitants in an area of 162km^2 (62sq miles), Brussels (Bruxelles in French; Brussel in Dutch) is composed of 19 *communes:* Anderlecht, Auderghem, Berchem-Sainte-Agathe, Bruxelles, Etterbeek, Evere, Forest, Ganshoren, Ixelles, Jette, Koekelberg, Molenbeek-Saint-Jean, Schaerbeek, Saint-Gilles, Saint-Josse-ten-Noode, Uccle, Watermael-Boitsfort, Woluwe-Saint-Lambert and Woluwe-Saint-Pierre. Bruxelles commune is the city's historic heart, lying mostly within the pentagonal inner ring road.

This central part, the Lower

City, around historic Grand-Place, occupies the bottom of a bowl-shaped depression reclaimed from marshes along the River Senne. The Upper City to the east runs from about the Royal Palace to Avenue Louise, though low hills also rise in other directions, to the heights of Anderlecht and Koekelberg in the west, and the Heysel plateau in the north. Southwards, in the direction of Waterloo, the Forêt de Soignes spreads a green canopy of leaves.

HISTORY

Beginnings

While western Europe flourished under the ancient **Romans**, the site on which Brussels would develop was a marshy cluster of islets in the River Senne, overlooked by a ring of low hills. It probably hosted a handful of farms. In 695, with the **Franks** in control, Bishop (later Saint) Gaugerich (Géry) of Cambrai apparently took refuge here and stayed until his death in 712.

Not until 966 do we have a documented reference to *Bruocsella*, meaning 'Settlement in the Marsh', which was slowly gaining importance as a crossing-point on the trade route from Bruges to Cologne. In 977, **Charles of France**, Duke of Lower Lotharingia (Lorraine), started work on a fortress on **Saint-Géry** island in the Senne. He occupied it in 979, giving the city its traditional foundation date. The relics of St Géry were housed in the fortress chapel, and in 985 were joined by the relics of St Gudule, a local martyr.

When Charles's son died in 1005, the counts of nearby Louvain (Leuven) inherited Brussels and ruled it for the next four centuries, during which time they also became dukes of Brabant. **Count Lambert II** took up residence in 1047 in a new fortress on higher ground, Coudenberg, and the town's relics of St Géry and St Gudule were moved

Godefroy de Bouillon, Duke of Lower Lorraine, led the First Crusade, and in July 1099 stormed Saracen-held Jerusalem.

from a chapel on Saint-Géry island to the new Church of Saint-Michel, named after the Archangel Michael, who became the town's patron saint (recent excavations under the cathedral have uncovered evidence of burials from around 900). In about 1100 work began on the first circuit of defensive walls, but the town soon outgrew them and began to spread up the surrounding hillsides. Brussels received its town charter in 1134.

Increasing prosperity from weaving and crafts allowed Brussels, in 1225, to start rebuilding the Church of Saint-Michel on a grander scale, as the **Church of Saints-Michel-et-Gudule**, elevated to cathedral status in 1961. In 1229 **Duke Henry I** granted the town its first written charter. Artisans and labourers who generated this wealth were, in 1303, driven to rebellion by low wages and appalling living conditions. They won seats on the town council, but in 1306 patrician forces, led by Duke John II of Brabant, crushed the rebels in battle at **Vilvoorde**. Following a brief occupation by troops of the Count of Flanders, work on a new wall to defend the expanding town began in 1357. It followed a pentagonal circuit, 8km (5 miles) in circumference, whose outline can be seen today in the shape of the city's inner ring road.

Burgundian Brussels

Despite a downturn in the cloth industry, the 15C began with a sure sign of Brussels' growing wealth when, in 1402, the foundation stone of a magnificent new **Town Hall** was laid in Grand-Place. The Burgundian period began in 1430, when the last Duke of Brabant, Philip I, died and

Duke Philip the Good of Burgundy, who already ruled Flanders in addition to his French realms, inherited Brabant. Brussels became the administrative centre of the Burgundian state, and amid growing prosperity developed a glittering court and a zest for the high life, at least among the upper classes, whose afterglow lingers in the description of modern Brussels as 'Burgundian'.

Artists flocked to the capital, most prominent among them the Flemish Primitives **Jan van Eyck** and **Rogier van der Weyden**, who in 1436 became the town's official artist. Tradesmen and craftsmen built opulent headquarters for their guilds in Grand-Place. The Burgundian adventure, during which the family acquired most of present-day Belgium, Holland and Luxembourg, came to an abrupt end in 1477 with the death in battle of **Duke Charles the Bold**, whose challenge to France's supremacy proved too bold for his own good. His daughter, **Mary of Burgundy**, was obliged to marry Crown Prince **Maximilian** of the Austrian Habsburg Empire, and when Mary died in a riding accident in 1482, Maximilian inherited the Burgundian territories, including Brussels.

The Habsburgs

Maximilian gave the Low Countries to his son Philip the Fair in 1494. Philip later married a Spanish princess, engagingly known as 'Joan the Mad', thereby creating the link with Spain that was later to cause much grief. Brussels temporarily lost its position as capital when Philip died in 1506, and his sister, Margaret of Austria, moved the court to Mechelen.

In 1515, it returned in style, when 15-year-old Archduke Charles of Brabant was proclaimed of age. Over the next few years, Charles became Holy Roman Emperor and took possession of the far-flung Habsburg lands in Austria, Spain, Italy, Germany, Hungary, the Low Countries and the Americas. As **Charles V**, he ruled from the Coudenberg Palace over an empire 'on which the sun never set', with Brussels serving as its *de facto* capital. The emperor's triumphal entry into the city in 1549 is recalled every year in the colourful *Ommegang* procession in Grand-Place.

The powerful Emperor Charles V (1500-58), 'on whose Empire the sun never set'.

During this period, in 1514, the anatomist **Vesalius** was born in Brussels; Jean-Baptiste de Tour et Taxis established an international postal service from the city in 1520; and Dutch humanist **Erasmus** lived in Anderlecht, then a village outside Brussels, in 1521, having lectured at the University of Leuven – he seems to have enjoyed his stay, and later, in Rotterdam, wrote: 'Oh, how I wish that Brabant was not so far away.'

Even when Charles abdicated in 1555 at the Coudenberg Palace in favour of his son, **Philip II**, Brussels retained much of its importance as government seat of the Low Countries. Chroniclers of the day describe it as a 'beautiful and great city'. In addition to monarchy and courtiers, it attracted church dignitaries, international merchants, along with philosophers, writers and artists, among them **Bruegel the Elder**, **Holbein** and **Dürer**.

The **Willebroek Canal**, dug from Brussels to the River Scheldt, gave the city an outlet to the sea.

Brussels' Golden Age drew to a close as chill winds of religious discord spread through the Low Countries in the wake of the Protestant Reformation. Philip, a fanatical Catholic, set out to suppress Protestantism. In 1567, he sent an army of 10 000 men led by the ruthless Spanish **Duke of Alva**, who established the Council of Troubles, better known as the Council of Blood, for the hundreds of executions it ordered. The following year **Counts Egmont** and **Hornes**, who had tried to deflect Alva's savagery while remaining loyal to Philip II, were beheaded in Grand-Place.

Full-scale rebellion erupted across the Low Countries. In 1577 Brussels was occupied by William of Orange and governed by Calvinists until 1585, when it was retaken by Spain. When the dust finally settled, the Netherlands was an independent, Protestant country, and Brussels was capital of the Spanish rump of the Low Countries, with Catholicism once more in the ascendant.

Tranquillity returned in 1599, after Philip appointed his daughter Isabella's husband, **Archduke Albert of Austria**, as ruler of what was now known as the Spanish Netherlands. After the tumultuous 16C, Brussels had a century of relative

Executed for their divided loyalties by Philip II, Counts Egmont and Hornes.

peace as capital of this backwater of the increasingly enfeebled Spanish Empire. Prosperity was slow to recover, and there was little improvement in ordinary people's already low standard of living.

The city's repose came to a crashing end on 13 August 1695, when **Maréchal de Villeroy**, commanding France's army in the Low Countries during the latest war with Spain, bombarded Brussels with cannonfire. The French gunners concentrated their fire on Grand-Place, using the Town Hall spire as a target marker, and pounded the historic square and its opulent wooden guildhouses to ruins – ironically they missed the Town Hall spire. The guildsmen refused to take this lying down, and within a few years had rebuilt their guildhouses in stone and on a grand scale, as you can see from a stroll around the square today.

Austrian Rule

Brussels' fate was once again bound up with distant dynastic struggles when the last Spanish Habsburg died and bequeathed his empire to a possible future heir to the French throne. The prospect of France and Spain uniting mobilised the other European powers to prevent it, and the War of the Spanish Succession (1700-13) ensued. When it ended, the Spanish Netherlands became at the stroke of a pen the Austrian Netherlands, under Emperor Charles VI.

Within a few years, the city was convulsed by rebellion against the Austrians, but the rebels were defeated and in 1719 their leader, **François Anneessens**, was executed. By the mid-18C, Brussels had almost 60 000 inhabitants, and by the end of the century its population had grown to more than

75 000. In 1731, when **Archduchess Marie-Elisabeth** was governor, the Coudenberg Palace, which dated from the 11C, was destroyed by fire. Charles's VI's death in 1740 provoked the War of the Austrian Succession, during which, in 1746, Brussels was occupied briefly by France.

The Austrian governor at this time was the popular **Charles of Lorraine**, and when things settled down on the political front he began to redevelop Brussels into an elegant regional capital, with Baroque and neo-Classical buildings, including his reconstruction of the Governor's Palace in what is now Place du Musée. Place Royale dates from this period.

At the foot of the Lion Mound, Waterloo, is a circular painting, 110m (358ft) in circumference, depicting the full-blooded French cavalry charge led by Marshal Ney.

Enter Napoleon

Austrian rule ended in fire and flame, firstly in a violent revolt by Brabant against the rigorous Austrian emperor, Joseph II. In 1790, the rebels proclaimed the United States of Belgium, but the new republic proved short-lived, with Austria re-establishing control in 1791. The following year, Revolutionary France invaded, and by 1795 Brussels was the capital of the French **Department of the Dyle** (named after the River Dijle that flows through Leuven and Mechelen).

Napoleon visited the city in 1803, and although some improvements in conditions for ordinary people were made, these were offset by military conscription and high taxation. The Napoleonic adventure came to a spectacular end in 1815 just south of Brussels, when Allied armies led by the Duke of Wellington and Marshal Blücher decisively defeated the emperor at the **Battle of Waterloo**.

Independence

Although Belgians now hoped for independence, the **Congress of Vienna** in 1814-15 decided to join the country to the Netherlands under King William I of Orange. Brussels became one of two seats of government, along with The Hague. The Dutch city clearly had the advantage, as the royal court remained there, though Brussels was the seat of diplomacy. In Belgium as a whole, the **industrial revolution** was advancing.

Brussels was the crucible of Belgium's **War of Independence**, which broke out on 25 August 1830 during a patriotic aria at an opera performance in the city's Théâtre Royal de la Monnaie. The following month

Dutch troops were defeated in a skirmish at the Parc de Bruxelles and the revolutionaries set up a provisional government. Within a year, the German **Prince Leopold of Saxe-Coburg-Gotha** had accepted an invitation to become King of the Belgians (1831-65) and was in Brussels taking his oath.

As though making up for too many centuries as part of other people's empires, Belgium moved quickly to make its mark. On May 5 1835, continental Europe's first **train service** made its inaugural journey from Mechelen to Brussels, and the capital quickly developed as the new nation's railway hub. A wave of building to bring the city up to capital standard included Europe's first shopping mall, the **Galeries Saint-Hubert**, which opened in 1847.

Under Leopold I's successor, his son **Leopold II** (1865-1909), the process continued. The polluted River Senne was covered over by graceful boulevards, and the monumental **Cinquantenaire** triumphal arch and museum complex, and the **Palais de Justice** were built. Apart from such monuments to national pride, the city embraced the exuberant turn-of-the-century Art Nouveau style, giving the genre one of its greatest exponents in the architect **Victor Horta**, and some of its most memorable works (*see* p.80).

Capital of Europe

Brussels' 20C journey to becoming Europe's *de facto* capital has not always been a smooth one. The city was occupied twice by Germany during both world wars (1914-18 and 1940-44). **King Albert I** (1909-34), the gallant 'Soldier King' of the First World War, returned to the Royal Palace at Laeken in triumph after leading the Belgian army's resistance. In sharp contrast, **King Leopold III** (1934-51) abdicated because of widespread, though not majority, public dissatisfaction with his Second World War role.

During the reigns of **King Baudoin I** (1951-93) and **Albert II** (1993-), the city has been a focal point of Europe's drive towards greater unity, first through the European Economic Community, then the European Community, and now the **European Union**. Brussels is headquarters of the **European Commission**, the civil service that administers EU programmes; home of the Council of Ministers; and one of the seats of the European Parliament. **NATO** has been established in the city since 1967. The

Brightly coloured national flags herald the European Parliament.

presence of such high-profile international institutions has brought in its train a plethora of diplomats, as well as business and lobbying organisations.

In 1958 the **World Fair** opened at the Parc des Expositions, dominated by the **Atomium**, a futuristic structure that has become a symbol of the city, and in 1979 Brussels celebrated its millennium. Since 1989 the city has been a region – Brussels Capital Region – in its own right, with its own government and parliament. As the new millennium begins, Brussels seems comfortable with its international role, if not always with the attendant side-effects. Having hosted empires, it is used to being a stage on which Europe's destiny is decided.

PEOPLE AND CULTURE

A strong case can be made for saying that Bruxellois are never happier than when they are settling down at a table in their favourite restaurant, reaching for the knife and fork, or when the setting changes to their favourite café, and an artisanal beer is about to put in an appearance. Eating out, if it does not quite have the character of a religion, is nevertheless a hallowed institution.

People expect to eat well and be properly served, whether they are splashing out a pile of thousand-franc notes for dinner at the top restaurant Comme Chez Soi (23 Place Rouppe) or ordering up the *plat du jour* at their neighbourhood café. The city's enviable 'Burgundian lifestyle' is most obvious in its restaurants.

Brussels is a city of neighbourhoods and when it comes to cafés, Bruxellois are faced with a hard choice of sticking with their friendly local watering-hole, or heading for one of the distinguished city-centre cafés to imbibe in Art Nouveau, Art Deco, or some other form of notable surroundings. The city's café society finds one of its sources in Belgium's hundreds of different beers, each one with its own particular design of glass (*see* p.105).

Euro-Brussels

When most Europeans think of the Capital of Europe, their eyes glaze over with images of rules and regulations, farm-support prices, and overpaid, overpowerful Eurocrats. The good news is that when most Bruxellois think of the Capital of Europe, their eyes glaze over for exactly the same reasons, and with even more justification, as they live in everyday proximity to the European Commission and all its works (and workers). So they do what citizens of this uniquely placed city have done with centuries-worth of starchy, alien overlords: ignore them and get on with the serious business of enjoying life. Few people are as good at that as Belgians.

Time Out

If there's one misconception that foreigners have of Brussels that produces bewildered stares from the Bruxellois themselves, it's the accusation that they and their city are somehow 'boring'. It's not easy to find evidence for this stereotype, and when you analyse its component parts they fade away before your eyes.

Brussels has about as much, and maybe more, opera, classical music and dance as you could expect in a city of a million people; it has a thriving theatre scene; plenty of cinema screens; a sufficiency of rock, jazz and blues venues; cabarets and nightclubs; no shortage of discos and dance clubs covering all the moves you care to make; there are more museums than you'll be able to visit on any reasonable timescale; fancy shopping; red light district; gay and lesbian scene; numerous characterful cafés and bars.

Have fun identifying the comic strip characters which feature on several buildings in the city.

What more do those who push the 'boring' myth want? That Bruxellois should dress up in funny clothes and parade through the streets? They do that as well, in historic processions and folklore rituals, in particular during the annual *Ommegang* on the Grand-Place, which evokes the extravagant event held on 2 June 1549 in the presence of Charles V. If you come to Brussels and find yourself complaining about being bored, you have only yourself to blame. People who live in this city don't have time to be bored; they're too busy simply enjoying themselves (and shrugging their shoulders at foreigners' misconceptions).

It's true that some parts of the city, overgrown with office blocks, have become little more than deserts with windows. The trick is to pass through these on the double, or better still avoid them in the first place, and get to where the action is. In any case, you are more likely to be impressed by the personality of the city's residential neighbourhoods. Not for the Bruxellois long rows of identical, production-line houses. Belgians are said to be born 'with a brick in their stomach', and their reverence for home shows up in the great number of *maisons de maître* – townhouses of such individuality that the architect's name is generally inscribed on the façade.

Language

Brussels is officially bilingual, its two languages being French and Dutch (Flemish is not a separate language, but a variant of the common language, *Nederlands*, spoken in the Netherlands and Flanders). Historically, it was a Flemish city, and indeed Brussels

Capital Region lies just inside the borders of contemporary Flanders – though it does not belong to Flanders – and not as you might expect along the boundary between Flanders and Wallonia. However, it is also evident that in more recent times, Brussels has been a mainly French-speaking city, with a substantial Dutch-speaking minority.

Given the political and cultural issues that preoccupy some sections of Belgian society, language can be a contentious issue in and around Brussels. Some Dutch speakers feel themselves to be a threatened minority. As always in Belgium, however, ordinary citizens generally get along much better than their political representatives. Many Bruxellois are happily bilingual and afford the 'other' language due respect.

An additional factor is the presence of a large expatriate community in the city, most of whose members, if they have to chose a Belgian language, prefer to learn and speak French because of its far greater international utility and the fact that many will already have studied French at school. Belgium's third official language is German, for the small German-speaking community in the east of the country. Brussels' *de facto* third language, though, is English. Many local people speak it to some extent and an impressive number are fluent. It's often used as a 'common' language between Dutch and French speakers.

French is likely to be the language you will use to fit in locally. Don't underestimate the charms of Dutch, though. If you try using a few words when you're in a Flemish environment (*see* p.119), you'll likely find your listeners more delighted than French speakers are when you speak French.

Surrealism in Brussels

In view of Brussels' reputation for bourgeois respectability, it seems surprising that the city embraced Surrealism so soon after the movement in art first made its appearance during the 1920s. Perhaps it should not be a surprise, as Brussels had already been introduced to 'Surrealism' during the 15C and 16C in the works of Hieronymous Bosch.

Among artists who embraced the movement, including **Paul Nougé** and **ELT Mesens**, the most notable was **René Magritte** (1898-1967), who had begun his career as a commercial artist, at one time designing wallpaper. Many of Magritte's paintings have a domestic feel, though subtly transmuted by his appeal to the subconscious, which may explain (or be explained by) the fact that he worked in his sitting room, rather than in a studio, in a perfectly respectable house, now the **Musée Magritte** (*see* p.75), in Jette, one of the city's suburban communes.

On the surface, Magritte's lifestyle seems a long way from that of an artist busily concocting a revolution in perception; he even wore a business suit while he worked. Yet his images – in works as diverse as *The Man in the Bowler Hat, The Rape,* and *The Natural Graces* – have an ability to unsettle and provoke that few artists have equalled, even when he is apparently only suggesting that a pipe he has painted is not a pipe, as, of course, it isn't. As a contributor to the journal *La Révolution Surrealiste,* he was fully aware of the significance of his ideas.

Paul Delvaux (1897-1989) – although he never accepted a Surrealist label for his work – was fully Magritte's equal, producing unsettling images that almost everyone else accepts as Surrealist, though with a realistic tinge. His subjects often include images of voyeurism and narcissism, with nude women pictured in classical urban scenes, often being observed by – and ignoring – respectable men in business suits.

MUST SEE

Grand-Place★★★

The historic Main Square, surrounded by 17C **guildhouses**, the Gothic **Hôtel de Ville** and neo-Gothic **Maison du Roi**, is still the city's heart today as it has been for centuries.

Le Cinquantenaire★★★ (Golden Jubilee)

The triumphalist architecture built to celebrate Belgium's independence Golden Jubilee in 1880 includes the **Arc du Cinquantenaire**, **Musée du Cinquantenaire★★★**, **Musée Royal de l'Armée et de l'Histoire Militaire** and **Autoworld★★**.

Musées Royaux des Beaux-Arts★★★
(Royal Fine Arts Museums)

The two art museums in this complex – **Musée d'Art Ancien★★★** and **Musée d'Art Moderne★★★** – combine to create a visual feast; the highlights are works by Belgian artists as diverse as Pieter Bruegel, Peter Rubens, René Magritte and Marcel Broodthaers.

Cathédrale des Saints-Michel-et-Gudule★★

The magnificent Gothic cathedral dates from 1226 but is built on the foundations of a centuries older church. Its white stone, twin towers and intricate exterior tracery contrast with a sober interior, to create a work of simplicity and grace.

You can spot it from a long way off, but nothing can quite prepare you for the impact of the Atomium close up.

Manneken Pis★★

Tiny sculpture of an irreverent little boy doing 'pee-pee' and grinning hugely at onlookers while doing so. There is no lack of onlookers and the statue has become the city's most recognisable symbol.

Quartier du Sablon** (Sablon Quarter)

Chic **Place du Grand-Sablon**, focus of the city's antiques business, is a place to see and be seen. Lounge on a café terrace and visit the excellent weekend antiques market. **Place du Petit-Sablon***, its smaller cousin, is built around a graceful little park surrounded by sculptures.

Musée Horta**

The house of the master of Art Nouveau, Victor Horta, is a remarkable example of the movement. Inside, the characteristic swirls and curving lines of Art Nouveau are reflected in the decor and furnishings.

Centre Belge de la Bande Dessinée** (Belgian Comic Strip Centre)

Belgium's fascination with, and creative bent for, comic strips is celebrated in a magnificent Art Nouveau setting. Tintin is the highlight, but there are many others.

Atomium*

This dramatic construction represents the atomic structure of iron. Built for the 1958 World Fair, it affords a magnificent view and has become a symbol of the city to rival the Manneken Pis.

Îlot Sacré (Sacred Isle)

The historic area around Grand-Place, mostly saved from demolition, is among the city's most characterful districts, filled with a vast array of international restaurants that justify its other name: the 'Stomach of Brussels'.

The neo-Gothic Maison du Roi, on Grand-Place, now houses the Brussels City Museum.

OLD CITY CENTRE

Grand-Place★★★ (Main Square) (JY)
Timeless, harmonious, **Grand-Place★★★** (Grote Markt in Dutch) is a world of its own, an island of calm perfection in the heart of a city that has often been cavalier with its architectural heritage. It is also, by any standard, one of the world's most beautiful squares. In 1998 Grand-Place was declared a World Cultural Heritage Site by UNESCO.

History seems to ooze up from its venerable cobblestones and wafts down from its gilded guildhouse façades, Gothic tracery and medieval banners. The square has witnessed everything: markets, riots, parades in honour of emperors, executions of scoundrels and popular heroes. In 1695 came its worst moment, when three days of French artillery bombardment reduced it to a smoking ruin. It was rebuilt within a few years on a grand scale and is now Brussels' theatre of life, a place of cafés and

Flower market in Grand-Place, with a row of guildhouses (from right to left, see Nos 1-6 opposite).

restaurants, snapshooting tourists, and modern events and festivals.

You may find it enough to view the square as an ensemble, taking in with a single sweep the astonishing harmony of its several architectural styles: Gothic, neo-Gothic, Flemish Renaissance, Italianate-Flemish, Louis XIV. If you look closer you will see a myriad details that add depth and character to the picture.

To see some of these, follow the house numbers around anticlockwise from the northern corner. At nos 1-2 is **Le Roi d'Espagne** (The King of Spain, 1696-97), formerly the Bakers Guildhouse and now a café. Above the entrance is a sculpture of St Aubert, patron saint of bakers, and above that medallions of Roman emperors Marcus Aurelius, Nerva, Decius and Trajan. The upper story has a bust of King Charles II of Spain flanked by a Moorish and a South

Map of the Guildhalls in Grand-Place

1-2 Le Roi d'Espagne
3 La Brouette
4 Le Sac
5 La Louve
6 Le Cornet
7 Le Renard
8 L'Étoile
9 Le Cygne
10 L'Arbre d'Or
11-12 La Rose and le Mont Thabor
13-19 Maison des Ducs de Brabant
20-23 Le Cerf, Joseph et Anne, l'Ange
24-25 La Chaloupe d'Or
26-27 Le Pigeon
28 La Chambrette de d'Amman
29-33 Maison du Roi
34-39 Le Heaume, le Paon, le Petit Renard et le Chêne, Sainte Barbe, l'Âne

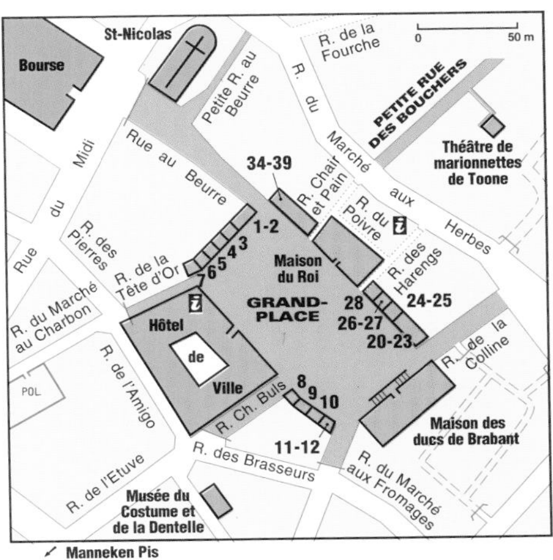

American Indian prisoner, and the rooftop dome is surmounted by a gilded statue representing Fame.

No 3, **La Brouette** (The Wheelbarrow, 1644-45), formerly the Tallow Merchants' Guildhouse and now a café, survived the 1695 bombardment and its façade was reworked in 1697. There is a cartouche decorated with a wheelbarrow, the tallow merchants' symbol, and a statue of St Gilles, their patron saint.

No 4, **Le Sac** (The Sack, 1645-46, restored 1697), was the Cabinet Makers' and Coopers' Guildhouse. Its extensive ornamentation includes a globe and compass symbol on the roof. No 5, **La Louve**

Savour your first glimpse of Grand-Place – ignore the many contemporary distractions around you and let your imagination float you back in time.

The Hôtel de Ville, with its magnificent spire, is the highlight of the square.

(The She-Wolf, 1696) was the Archers' Guildhouse. The name comes from a bas-relief above the entrance of a she-wolf suckling Romulus and Remus. No 6, **Le Cornet** (The Horn, 1697), was the Boatmen's Guildhouse; its gable recalls the stern of a sailing ship. No 7, **Le Renard** (The Fox, 1699), was the Haberdashers' Guildhouse, and has bas-reliefs of cherubs doing typical haberdashery tasks and a rooftop statue of St Nicholas, patron saint of haberdashers.

Undoubted star of the show is the **Hôtel de Ville** (Town Hall), whose soaring, 96m (312ft) spire topped by a gilded statue of the Archangel Michael, the city's patron, is now free of the renovators' scaffolding that disfigured it for years. Work began in 1401 on a town hall worthy of a wealthy and influential city. Its south wing and belfry were completed in 1421. The north wing, shorter than its companion, was added between 1444 and 1459, and a spire added to the off-centre belfry. You can tour the building to see the tapestried Council Chamber, where the Brabant Estates once sat. Tourist Information Brussels (TIB) is on the ground floor.

On the corner of Rue Charles Buls is a bronze recumbent statue of Everard 't Serclaes, a popular guild leader executed in 1356 by the Count of Flanders. Across the street is no 8, **L'Étoile** (The Star, 1695),

Lay your hands on the 'lucky' bronze statue of Everard 't Serclaes in the passageway of L'Étoile to ensure your good fortune.

the square's smallest building. Next door, no 9, **Le Cygne** (The Swan, 1698), was a private house that in 1720 became the Butchers' Guildhouse, and is now La Maison du Cygne, a top-flight restaurant. Karl Marx and Friedrich Engels met here to discuss *The Communist Manifesto.* No 10, **L'Arbre d'Or** (The Golden Tree, 1698), surmounted by a gilded statue of Duke Charles of Lorraine, houses the Brewers' Guild, Belgian Brewers Confederation and, in a reconstructed 18C café, the **Musée de la Brasserie** (Brewery Museum). Nos 11 and 12 are, respectively, **La Rose** (The Rose, 1702) and **Le Mont Thabor** (Mount Thabor, 1699), two graceful private homes.

The Grand-Place's southern face, nos 13-19, is occupied by the palatial **Maison des Ducs de Brabant** (House of the Dukes of Brabant, 1698), six former guildhouses together in a group. The **Musée du Chocolat** has recently opened at no 13.

The Maison des Ducs de Brabant is named after the 19 busts of the Dukes on the façade.

On the east side, nos 20-23, **Le Cerf** (The Stag, 1710), **Joseph et Anna** (1700) and **L'Ange** (The Angel, 1697) are private houses. Nos 24-25, **La Chaloupe d'Or** (The Golden Sloop, 1697), used to be the Tailors' Guildhouse and is now a café. A bust of St Barbara, patron saint of tailors, stands above the doorway, while St Boniface blesses passers-by from the roof – look closely and you will notice he lacks a vital item of clothing. Victor Hugo lived during 1851 at nos 26-27, **Le Pigeon** (1697), formerly the Painters' Guildhouse. No 28, **La Chambrette d'Amman** (The Mayor's Chamber, 1709), was an office of the Duke of Brabant's city magistrate.

The **Maison du Roi** (King's House), nos 29-33, has its symmetries better arranged than the Town Hall opposite, as you might expect from a neo-Gothic building of 1873. It houses the **Musée de la Ville de Bruxelles** (Brussels City Museum) which traces the city's history using artefacts, models, paintings and photographs; these include fascinating images of an early, Venice-like city, clustered on islands in the Senne. There are some 600 costumes, donated by governments, associations and individuals to Manneken Pis, which the little fellow wears on special occasions.

The last buildings in this trip around Grand-Place are nos 34-39, a group of relatively plain houses called **Le Heaume**, **Le Paon**, **Le Petit Renard et Le Chêne**, **Sainte Barbe**, and **L'Âne**.

The Maison du Roi provides a perfect backdrop for the colourful pageants and tourist displays staged in the Grand-Place.

Around Grand-Place

There is much more to the centre than the Grand-Place itself. For a taste of the centre's hustle and bustle, leave Grand-Place by Rue Charles Buls and turn left into Rue de la Violette to visit the **Musée du Costume et de la Dentelle** (Costume and Lace Museum) (JY M[14]) at no 6, and its fine collection of antique lace pieces and clothes. Go left along Rue des Eperonniers to Place d'Espagne, where a **crafts market** is held at the weekend; beside the fountain 'sits' a moustachioed sculpture of the 19C mayor, Charles Buls.

Take the right fork into Rue de la Madeleine to the pretty Gothic **Chapelle de la Madeleine** (Magdalene Chapel), rebuilt after the 1695 bombardment. **Galerie Bortier**, a shopping gallery dating from 1848, is in the middle of the next block; stroll through this elegant arcade, filled with secondhand bookshops. Turn right into Rue Saint-Jean; at the busy traffic intersection at its end, go left to **Place de la Vieille Halle-aux-Blés**, a graceful little square. At no 11, the **Fondation Brel** (Brel Foundation) (JZ F[8])

Map of Bruxelles

B Appartements de Ch. de Lorraine
E[1] Colonne du Congrès
F[3] Église N.-D.-du Finistère
F[5] Église St-Jean-Baptiste-au-Béguinage
F[7] Église Sts-Jean-et-Étienne-aux-Minimes
F[8] Fondation Brel
H Hôtel de Ville
I[2] Hôtel Métropole
I[3] Hôtel Ravenstein
M[2] Musée d'Art Moderne
M[4] Musée Bibliothèque Royale de Belgique
M[5] Musée Bruxella 1238
M[8] Musée Centre belge de la Bande dessinée
M[10] Musée du Cinéma
M[14] Musée du Costume et de la Dentelle
M[21] Old England: Musée des Instruments de Musique
M[24] Musée des Postes et des Télécommunications
M[28] Musées Bellevue
Q[1] Palais des Beaux-Arts
Q[2] Palais des Congrès
Q[3] Palais de la Dynastie
S Statue équestre de Léopold II
T[2] Théâtre de marionnettes de Toone
V[1] Tour Anneessens
V[2] Tour de Villers
V[3] Tour Noire
V[4] Tour de l'ancienne église Ste-Catherine
W Vitrine de P. Hankar

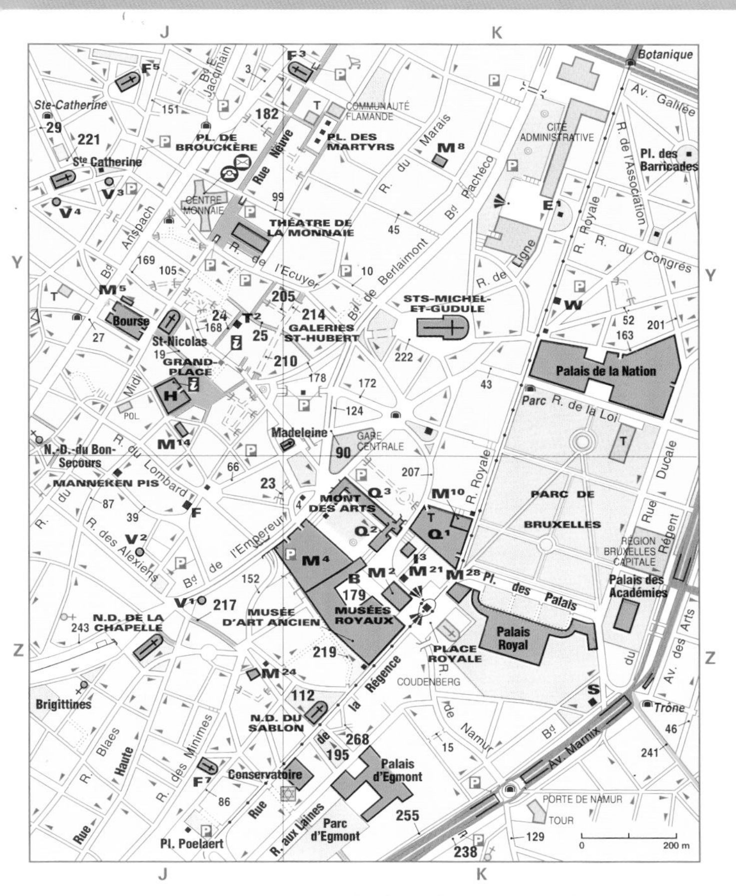

Left: Ex-mayor Charles Buls perches beside the fountain in Place d'Espagne.

recounts the life of the great Belgian singer/songwriter Jacques Brel (1929-78).

Go downhill on Rue du Chêne, making a short detour to the left into Rue de Villers to see the **Tour de Villers** (JZ V^2), one of few surviving towers from the 12C city wall. Look

The solid, Classical bulk of La Bourse is decorated with an extravaganza of sculptures.

for the building on the left which is decorated with the famous comic strip characters Dany and Greg. On the corner of Rue de l'Etuve you will probably find a crowd gathered in front of **Manneken Pis**★★ (JZ), Brussels' famous city mascot, a small fountain-sculpture of a little boy doing with joyful panache what comes naturally. He may be wearing one of the 600 or so costumes kept in the Brussels City Museum, or he may be *au naturel.* 'Little Julian' has been doing his business diligently since 1619 but the current performer is a replica, as the original has been stolen and damaged several times, though always recovered. The old **Poechenellekelder** café opposite displays a collection of theatre marionettes.

At the next corner a block further downhill, turn right into Rue du Midi, a street known for its coin and stamp dealers, until you arrive at **La Bourse** (Stock

Exchange) (JY). This colonnaded and heavily ornamented temple of capitalism in beige stone dates from 1868-73. You can watch the money gurus at work from behind a glass screen. As you stroll around the ornate exterior, look into the Art Nouveau **Le Falstaff** café in Rue Henri Maus and the faded *fin-de-siècle* opulence of **Le Cirio** café in Rue de la Bourse. Also in this street is the small **Bruxella 1238** (JY M[5]) archaeological museum, on the site of a demolished Franciscan monastery founded in 1238.

Take your pick from the wealth of excellent restaurants in the old city centre.

On the corner of Rue de Tabora and Rue au Beurre stands the **Église Saint-Nicolas** (Church of St Nicholas), whose origins date back to the founding of the city, although the present construction dates from after the 1695 bombardment. Among its treasures is a painting, *Virgin and Child Asleep*, attributed to Rubens.

Go up Rue du Marché-aux-Herbes and turn left into **Petite Rue des Bouchers**★ (JY 24), to the heart of the **Îlot Sacré** restaurant district, with pavement terraces and seafood displays all around. Midway along make a short detour into Impasse Schuddeveld; at the end is **Théâtre de Marionnettes de Toone** (JY T^2), a traditional café-cum-puppet theatre whose performances are often in Brussels dialect, *Brusseleir*, but whose action makes dialogue all but superfluous.

Head for Galeries Saint-Hubert, one of the more distinguished sights in Brussels, with its vaulted glass ceiling. Enjoy a pleasant stroll around its elegant luxury shops, or simply while away the time in one of the pavement cafés.

Turn right into Rue des Bouchers – a brief detour in the other direction, to Impasse de la Fidelité, reveals **Jeanneke Pis**, the modern female counterpart of Manneken Pis – and continue through the restaurant district until you reach the **Galeries Saint-Hubert**★★ (St Hubert Galleries) (KY), a magnificent shopping arcade from 1846-47. There are three galleries in this elegant Italian neo-Renaissance complex – **Galerie du Roi**, **Galerie de la Reine** and **Galerie des Princes** – lined with chic shops, cafés and restaurants.

At the end of Rue des Bouchers turn left

The twin towers of the Cathédrale des Saints-Michel-et-Gudule soar into the darkness of the night sky.

The cathedral has some fine stained-glass windows.

into Rue de la Montagne, and cross Boulevard de l'Impératrice to the **Cathédrale des Saints-Michel-et-Gudule★★** (Cathedral of St Michael and St Gudule) (KY). Its white stonework beautifully restored, the Gothic cathedral dates from the start of the 13C to the end of the 15C, having replaced a Romanesque church of 1047 to which Count Lambert II of Louvain had moved the relics of St Gudule. Recent excavations have uncovered the crypt and chapter house of the earlier church. The cathedral's twin towers soar 69m (222ft) and are unusual since Brabant architecture usually dictates a single tower. Its vast interior is relatively plain. There are tombs of Duke John II of Brabant and other dignitaries of Brabant, Burgundy and the Habsburg Empire, and among its fine stained-glass windows is *The Last Judgement* dating from 1528.

Monnaie Quarter★★

Brussels' opera and dance venue, the **Théâtre Royal de la Monnaie★** (Royal Mint Theatre) (JY), in Place de la Monnaie, has a powerful claim to distinction – it inspired a revolution. Belgium's 1830 national revolt against Dutch rule, complete with musketry, cannonfire and patriot dead, began here on 25 August 1830 during a performance of the opera *The Mute Girl of Portici.* The audience, fired up by an aria about freedom and patriotism, rushed into the street bent on making life imitate art. Within a year, Prince Leopold of Saxe-Coburg-Gotha was crowned King of the Belgians. Only the neo-Classical peristyle of eight Ionic columns, topped by a pediment, remain of the original 1817-19 building, which was rebuilt after being badly damaged by fire in 1855.

Facing La Monnaie, beyond a modern fountain is the **Centre Monnaie**, a busy shopping mall. The pavement terrace of the traditional, wood-panelled and mirrored

Not just a place to hear the opera, the Théâtre Royal de la Monnaie was the launchpad of the 1830 War of Independence.

La Lunette café at 3 Place de la Monnaie makes a good place for soaking up the atmosphere while imbibing La Lunette beer from a wide-brimmed, 1-litre glass.

Cross Rue du Fossé-aux-Loups to **Rue Neuve** (JKY), a popular pedestrianised shopping street, where window-shopping is a pleasure, then turn left through Passage du Nord shopping gallery. This brings you neatly to the **Hôtel Métropole**, 31 Place de Brouckère. The *belle époque* hotel has been fashionable since it opened in 1894, and its lavishly decorated **Café Métropole** has featured in films. Three boulevards converge on the square, which is rich in 1870s French Second Empire architecture.

Go north along Boulevard Adolphe Max to Rue du Finistère, and turn right, passing the Art Deco L'Espérance café, to the Baroque **Église Notre-Dame-du-Finistère**, from 1708-30, which seems lost in the middle of a busy shopping district. The church's ornate interior has three white marble altars.

Turn off Rue Neuve into Rue Saint-Michel to **Place des Martyrs★** (Martyrs' Square) (KY). Only a few years ago, its neo-Classical 18C buildings and memorial to 445 dead heroes of Belgium's 1830 Revolution were dilapidated and in serious danger of falling down. Restoration has given the square back its surface grace, though in the process most of its mansions have been reduced to their shells by interior demolition, then rebuilt and turned into offices.

Leave the square by Rue du Persil on its east side, then turn left into Rue du Marais and right into Rue des Sables, to the **Centre Belge de la Bande Dessinée★★** (Belgian Comic Strip Centre) (KY M^8) at no 20. The

first thing you notice is the splendid setting, in the former **Magasins Waucquez**, an Art Nouveau textile warehouse and shop, from 1903-06, by Victor Horta. Doomed to be demolished, it was saved during the 1980s by a popular outcry and converted into this wonderful museum and research centre reflecting Belgium's passion for comic strips – the 'Ninth Art'. At the top of a marble staircase, lit through a wrought-iron-and-glass skylight, you come to a model of Tintin's red-and-white moon rocket. Other comic-strip heroes are celebrated, too, including Lucky Luke, the Smurfs, and Bob and Bobette. Modern, realistic strips, and erotic strips, are also featured (*see* p.44).

Eating moules et frites is a cliché but a good way to taste the Belgians' soul.

Comic Strips

Belgium is a big player in the comic strip industry, producing 30 million books a year and exporting 75 per cent of them. A Brussels museum, the **Belgian Comic Strip Centre★★** (*see* p.42), takes a lofty view of the 'Ninth Art', and characters decorate gable ends and metro stations in the city. Comic book enthusiasts will especially enjoy following the **trail** through the city which visits a series of these buildings decorated with famous comic strip characters. A brochure indicating the exact location of these murals can be obtained from the Tourist Information Office in Grand-Place.

Tintin first appeared in the Belgian newspaper *Le Petit Vingtième* in 1929, in black-and-white and without his trademark quiff, in *Tintin in the Land of the Soviets.* Tintin's creator, the Belgian Georges Rémi – whose initials, reversed and written as they would be pronounced in French, come out as **Hergé** – produced 24 adventures.

Like all good comic strip characters, Tintin has become timeless – France's General de Gaulle once described him as his greatest rival. He quarters the globe, doing good, accompanied by blustery Captain Haddock and his faithful dog Snowy. More than 200 million copies of the *Tintin* books have been published, in just about every language under the sun.

A dark side of the force shines through in **Thorgal**. Displacement and *anomie* characterise the stories – although the attractions of a good fight are not ignored. Thorgal Aegirsson, born in outer space and sent to Earth by his mother after his father and grandfather quarrelled over whether or not to invade the planet, lives during the

Viking era. He knows how to use broadsword and battleaxe to defend himself, his wife Aarcia and their two children.

One of Belgium's most popular strips, **Suske en Wiske**, began in 1945. Since then, 200 full length stories have been published. Unlike strips that use children to make points about adult life, the child heroes take part in adventures that have a life of their own. *Suske en Wiske's* popularity has spread beyond Belgium: the series is published in English as *Willy and Wanda*, in French as *Bob et Bobette.*

Above: 'Boule and Bill' cartoon, Rue du Chevreuil.
Left: Cartoon on the end of a building, Rue des Capucins.
Below: The Belgian Comic Strip Centre.

Ville Ancienne (Old City) (JY)
Across Boulevard Anspach from the Bourse is where Brussels began, along the marshy banks of the **River Senne**, but where is the River Senne? It was banished underground between 1867 and 1871, after its polluted waters had been linked to an 1866 cholera epidemic in which 3 467 died. Islands that had given Brussels a Bruges-like character were linked together and built over.

The area has a raffish, bohemian character. At the heart of the old city is **Place Saint-Géry**, a former island in the Senne on which, between 977 and 979, Duke Charles of Lower Lorraine built the fortress around which Brussels grew. In 1881 a covered market, **Les Halles Saint-Géry** (ER), was built here. Restored during the early 1990s, it houses an exhibition space and café and is the focus of a trendy nightlife scene in the cafés and restaurants round about. There are also notorious examples of 'façadisation', a Brussels practice in which a valuable old building's interior is demolished, leaving its façade to be 'redeveloped'. You can catch a glimpse of the bricked-over River Senne behind the cobbled courtyard of the tavern **Le Lion d'Or**, facing the Halles.

From Place Saint-Géry take Rue de la Grande-Île which brings you, in Rue des Riches-Claires, to the Italianate-Flemish, late-17C **Église Notre-Dame-des-Riches-Claires** (Church of Our Lady of the Riches-Claires), belonging to a convent that is still being restored after being heavily damaged in 1989 by fire.

From here walk along Rue Saint-Christophe, to the fascinating **Album** museum (25 Rue des Chartreux) (ER M[1]), founded in 1997 by Frenchman Olivier

Guilbaud. In this well-restored 17C house, the new interactive 'Europe zig-zag' exhibition provides an enjoyable way to learn more about various aspects of Europe.

Take Rue du Vieux Marché-aux-Grains – which crosses Rue Antoine Dansaert, lined with stylish boutiques, and chic **L'Archiduc** café at no 6 – to a tree-lined square at its end. **Le Paon Royal** at no 6 is a fine, traditional Brussels restaurant.

Place Sainte-Catherine

Among the city's most characterful areas is **Place Sainte-Catherine** (JY), laid out in 1870 on the filled-in basin of the old port that once joined the Willebroek Canal and connected with the River Scheldt near Antwerp. Old warehouses and gabled houses in the surrounding streets testify to the area's former role and wealth.

All that remains of a 14C-17C church that stood in the square until 1850 is a Baroque tower. It now forms the belfry of the 1854 **Église Sainte-Catherine** (Church of St Catherine), designed by Joseph Poelaert of Justice Palace fame (*see* p.61), though this has a far lighter touch than his monstrous legal masterpiece. La Sirène d'Or seafood restaurant in the square is excellent. Facing the church, the **Tour Noire** (Black Tower) (JY V[3]) is a rare surviving element from the 12C city wall, now incorporated into the wall of a Novotel hotel.

At right angles to this square is the long and atmospheric **Marché-aux-Poissons** (Fish Market): two rectangular pools stand in for the vanished port and the former shipping quays, Quai-aux-Briques and Quai-aux-Bois-à-Brûler, are the setting for a cluster of seafood restaurants which set up outdoor tables in good weather. Between the pools is a fountain.

From the eastern side of the Fish Market, take Rue du Peuplier to the richly-decorated Baroque **Église Saint-Jean-Baptiste-au-Béguinage** (Church of St John the Baptist-in-the-Beguinage), from 1657-76. The tranquil district around here used to be the location of the city's Beguinage, founded in 1250 as a religious community for pious single women who did not take nuns' vows. Now it holds the **Institut Pachéco** (EQ), a hospice for convalescents.

Return to Place Sainte-Catherine via a short detour into Rue de Laeken to see, at no 146, the neo-Baroque **Koninklijke Vlaamse Schouwburg** (Royal Flemish Theatre) (EQ T[1]), patronised by the city's Dutch-speaking theatre-goers; it occasionally hosts performances in English (currently undergoing restoration).

RUE ROYALE (ROYAL ROAD) (FQR)

Le Botanique District (FQ)

Take tram 90, 92, 93 or 94 to Place de la Reine at the northern end of Rue Royale, easily identified by the green-domed **Église Sainte-Marie** in the middle of the square. The octagonal church (1845) was inspired by the 6C Byzantine Basilica di San Vitale in Ravenna, Italy. A few steps away, in Rue Royale Sainte-Marie, are the **Halles de Schaerbeek**, a 19C covered market, renovated during the 1980s and now a performing arts venue.

Go south along Rue Royale, past the Art Nouveau café-restaurant **De Ultieme Hallucinatie** at no 316, in a 1904 townhouse by Paul Hamesse. This brings you to **Le**

Botanique*, formerly the Botanical Garden, laid out between 1826 and 1830. Its neo-Classical, domed, iron-and-glass greenhouse is now home to the Centre Culturel de la Communauté Française, and hosts exhibitions, theatre, concerts and other events. The gardens extend west towards Place Rogier and, though hemmed in by busy roads, still make for a pleasant walk.

Further on, past the modern **Cité Administrative** government offices, you come to the belle époque **Astoria Hotel**, dating from 1909; drop in to its Pullman Bar, modelled on the 1920s Orient Express restaurant. Across the street an eternal flame honouring Belgium's First World War dead burns at the **Tomb of the Unknown Soldier**, beneath the **Colonne du Congrès** (Congress Column) (KY E[1]). The 47m (153ft) column, built in 1859 by Joseph Poelaert, commemorates the country's post-independence

Attractive formal gardens front Le Botanique, now a French Cultural Centre.

constitutional convention and is topped by a **statue** of King Léopold I. Look out for **Chocolatier Mary's** luscious handmade pralines at no 73, and for the 1896 Art Nouveau **shopfront*** by Paul Hankar – the city's last surviving example – of florist Les Fleurs Isabelle de Baecker at no 13 (KYW).

Gone, but not forgotten, the Tomb of the Unknown Soldier commemorates the First World War dead.

Parliament District (KYZ)
You come next to the **Palais de la Nation** (Palace of the Nation), Belgium's national parliament building. Despite having ceded slices of power to the regions (Brussels Capital, Flanders, Wallonia) and cultural communities (French, Dutch, German), both houses of parliament, Senate and Chamber of Representatives, still have plenty to say for themselves, as you can hear by attending a debate (telephone in advance for details ☎ **02 549 81 36**). Several rooms can be visited, and the finely decorated Senate Session Room is especially worth a look.

Quieter relaxation is on offer over the way in the **Parc de Bruxelles*** (Brussels Park). Currently undergoing renovations, this remnant of a former royal hunting estate is an 18C French garden with fountains, neo-Classical statuary, and woods. In good weather it is full of joggers, sunbathers and strolling civil servants. The graceful **Théâtre Royal du Parc**, in the north-east corner, was severely damaged by fire in 1998 and is closed for repairs.

Place des Palais at the park's southern end is lined by three palaces. On the western side is the **Palais des Beaux-Arts** (Fine Arts Palace) (KZ Q[1]), an arts centre designed by Victor Horta in Art Deco style, dating from 1923-28. It hosts art exhibitions, concerts and theatre. To the east is the neo-Classical **Palais des Académies** (Palace of the Academies, 1823), once the Prince of Orange's residence and now the headquarters of scientific, philosophical and literary societies. At the end of the short Rue Ducale beside this palace stands an equestrian statue of **King Léopold II** (KZ S).

On the square's southern edge is the **Palais Royal** (Royal Palace), on which the Belgian flag flies when King Albert is in residence – it is his office, the main royal

Once the stage for jousting tournaments, the Parc de Bruxelles is now a haven for residents and visitors alike.

residence being the Laeken Palace (*see* p.76). Built after 1815 on the orders of King William I, when Belgium was part of the Netherlands, it has since been extended and extensively remodelled. You can generally visit between July and September (closed Mondays), and admire the royal apartments and chambers with their fine furniture, tapestries, the grand staircase by A Balat and his great reception rooms, the highlight of which is the grandiose **Throne Room**.

The splendid apartments of the **Hôtel Bellevue**, an annexe of the Royal Palace on the corner of Rue Royale, house the **Musée de la Dynastie** (Dynasty Museum), featuring memorabilia of the Belgian royal family from 1831 to the present day.

The national flag flies over the Palais Royal when the King of Belgium is in residence.

Place Royale★

Rue Royale runs into emblematic **Place Royale★** (KZ) and continues on the other side as Rue de la Régence. In the middle is a triumphant equestrian statue from 1848 of **Godefroy de Bouillon**, Duke of Lower Lorraine. Godefroy led the First Crusade, which in July 1099 stormed Saracen-held Jerusalem (*see* p.8).

Behind Godefroy stands the neo-Classical **Église Saint-Jacques-sur-Coudenberg** (Church of St James-on-Coudenberg), which looks like a Roman temple; on the steps, Prince Leopold of Saxe-Coburg-Gotha took the oath of office in 1831 to become Léopold I, King of the Belgians.

Place Royale stands on Coudenberg, a hill

The unusual Classical pillared façade of the Église Saint-Jacques-sur-Coudenberg faces the Place Royale.

the medieval Counts of Louvain chose as a more defensible position for their Brussels residence than the original site on low-lying Saint-Géry island. The Dukes of Brabant and Burgundy and the Habsburg emperors (Charles V abdicated here) extended the **Coudenberg Palace** and made it more luxurious. All this came to an abrupt end when the palace was consumed by fire during February 1731. With water supplies frozen, the firefighters apparently tried quenching the flames with beer – to no avail. You can see excavations of the cellars of the once magnificent palace in the north-west corner of the square.

A short way downhill on Rue Montagne de la Cour is the magnificent former **Old England*** (KZ N) department store, an Art Nouveau extravaganza of wrought-iron arabesques and glass designed by Paul Saintenoy, built in 1899 and recently restored. Since June 2000 it has housed the **Musée des Instruments de Musique**** (Musical Instruments Museum) and its collection of 6 000 musical instruments.

Musées Royaux des Beaux-Arts***
(Royal Fine Arts Museums) (KZ)

These two outstanding, connected museums – **Musée d'Art Ancien***** (Ancient Art Museum) and **Musée d'Art Moderne***** (Modern Art Museum) (M²) – are your first ports of call. Although many international artists are represented (French, Dutch, German, Italian and Spanish), Belgian works form the core of both collections.

The **Ancient Art Museum** united several collections, including works endowed by Napoleon I. It begins with paintings by the 15C 'Flemish Primitives' and moves up, on the *blue tour*, through the centuries, to paintings of the 16C. You can see masterpieces by, among others, Petrus Christus, Rogier van der Weyden, Hans Memling, Hieronymous Bosch, Pieter Bruegel the Elder and Pieter Bruegel the Younger. The *brown tour* includes Peter Paul Rubens, van Dyck and Jacob Jordaens, and Dutch masters such as Rembrandt and Frans Hals.

The **Modern Art Museum** is underground – you can look into the hemicyclical museum, which opened in 1984, from a light well on the surface in Place du Musée.

Elegance and style abound in the restored Old England department store, now the Musical Instruments Museum.

On a descending tour of its eight levels you can admire collections of 20C sculptures, paintings and drawings, which are arranged more or less in chronological order. As there is much to see, you are advised to select the levels which correspond to your particular interests rather than attempt a whistle-stop tour of everything.
For the 19C follow the yellow tour:
Level –2: Neo-Classical and Romantic schools, including Jacques-Louis David.
Level –1: Realist movement, including Gustave Courbet, Henri de Braekeleer.
Level 1: Realist movement and Belgium's famous representative Constantin Meunier.
Level 2: Belgian and foreign neo-Impressionists and luminists: Anna Boch, Henry van de Velde, Émile Claus, and Symbolist Fernand Khnopff.
Level 3: Paintings of James Ensor and French artists including Gauguin, Bonnard.
For the 20C follow the green tour:
Level –3: Includes various international artists such as Pol Bury and Francis Bacon, and is part of the Goldschmidt collection donated to the museum.
Level –4: Fauvists, Cubists, Abstract and Expressionist, including Rik Wouters, Léon Spilliaert, Victor Servranckx, Marc Chagall, Constant Permeke.
Level –5: Surrealism, including Paul Colinet, Marcel Mariïn, ELT Mesens, Paul Nougé, Raoul Ubac, Jean Scutenaire.
Level –6: Georgette and René Magritte room; Post-war Abstract art and other new movements.
Level –7: Various modern trends of the 1960s.
Level –8: Post 1960s artists.
Note that although the museum is open from 10am to 5pm, the blue and yellow tours are closed

between noon and 1pm and the brown and green tours between 1pm and 2pm.

A few steps along the road from the museum complex is the **Jardin de Sculpture**, where you can sit and rest tired feet while still looking at works of art.

Admiring a Rubens, one of the great artists represented in the Musée d'Art Ancien.

Mont des Arts*

South-east of Grand-Place, and connecting the Lower City with the Upper City around Place du Musée and Place Royale is the **Mont des Arts*** (KZ), intended by King Léopold II to be the focus of a 19C arts museum district. It never developed that way and, during the 1950s and 1960s, the park on the site was remodelled.

Skateboarders now enjoy the marble esplanade, on which stands an **equestrian statue** of King Albert I, as it makes a perfect surface for their manoeuvres. King Albert gazes across busy Boulevard de l'Empereur to Place de l'Albertine, where his wife, Queen Elisabeth, is depicted in a less heroic though more graceful sculpture.

Behind Albert, a shady ornamental garden with a fountain at its end is bordered by the 1969 **Bibliothèque Royale de Belgique** (Royal Library of Belgium), which houses historic manuscripts and a vast number of Belgian and international books and publications. Part of the collection is housed in the splendid Louis XVI **Appartements de Charles de Lorraine** (Charles of Lorraine Apartments) (KZ B), the recently restored palace of the 18C governor of the Austrian Low Countries, in adjacent Place du Musée (*see* p.55).

Across the park is the 1950s **Palais des Congrès** (Congress Palace) (KZ Q[2]) conference and exhibition centre and **Palais de la Dynastie** (Dynasty Palace) (KZ Q[3]) – look on the rear façade for a clock with

The equestrian statue of King Albert I is by A Courtens.

12 mechanical figures representing historical and folkloric characters.

On adjacent Rue Ravenstein, the **Hôtel Ravenstein**, the city's last surviving 15C Burgundian mansion, houses professional institutes and a fine restaurant, the Relais des Caprices.

Sablon Quarter**

Passing back through the Musées Royaux to Place Royale, keep going along Rue de la Régence for a short distance until you come to two adjacent squares separated by the road. To your right is **Place du Grand-Sablon** (JKZ 112), whose entrance is partly filled by a Flamboyant Gothic church usually known

Fine buildings surround the ornamental gardens, Mont des Arts.

as the **Église Notre-Dame du Sablon★**, though its full name is the Église Notre-Dame-des-Victoires (Our Lady of Victories). Built in the 15C and 16C, it replaced the 12C chapel of the city's Guild of Crossbowmen. Look out in particular for the magnificent stained-glass rose window with a Madonna and Child at its heart.

The elegant bustling Place du Grand-Sablon has plenty of ambience, thanks to its restaurants and cafés with pavement terraces, tony art and antique shops, and a superb weekend antiques market. **Wittamer** cake and praline shop at no 12-13 and **Le Pain Quotidien** bakery and tearoom at no 11 are both excellent. England's Lord Aylesbury donated the **Fountain of Minerva**, at the lower end of the square, in gratitude for the warm treatment he received during his exile in the city. Philately and telephone buffs should enjoy the **Musée des Postes et des Télécommunications** (JZ M[24]).

The Flamboyant Gothic Église Notre-Dame du Sablon is the starting point of the Ommegang procession.

On the other side of Rue de la Régence, **Place du Petit-Sablon★** (KZ 195) is quite different – a charming little garden laid out in the 1890s and surrounded by 48 columns topped by sculptures of medieval guildsmen. The central fountain is fronted by statues of Counts Egmont and Hornes, executed in 1568 by the Spanish. At the top of the square, the **Palais d'Egmont** (Egmont Palace), originally 16C but altered and extended since then, houses Belgium's Ministry of Foreign Affairs. To visit the handsome **Parc d'Egmont** (Egmont Park), formerly the palace's gardens, you need to make a detour along Rue aux Laines to Rue du Grand-Cerf.

One of the bronze statues of medieval guildsmen in the Place du Petit-Sablon.

Pass the **Conservatoire Royal de Musique** (Royal Music Conservatory) at no 30 and, next door, the 180-year-old main **Synagogue**, on your way to the **Palais de Justice** (Justice Palace) (ES J), at the end of Rue de la Régence. To call the Justice Palace 'colossal' is to understate the case. One of Europe's largest buildings, this domed temple encloses an area of 26 000m² (279 760sq ft), and seems to go beyond glorifying the might and majesty of the law to being a statement of architectural intimidation. Designed by Joseph Poelaert, who (perhaps not surprisingly) collapsed and died during its construction, and built between 1866 and 1887 on the Galgenberg Hill, once occupied by the city gallows, it looms menacingly above the working-class Marolles district. You get a fine view of the Marolles from the esplanade of Place Poelaert, in the middle of which stands a **monument** to the First World War Belgian infantry.

Place du Petit-Sablon – an elegant islet of green on a 'royale' avenue bordered with magnificent monuments.

Continuing past the front of the Justice Palace, along Rue des Quatre-Bras, brings you to busy Place Stéphanie. This leads to upmarket shops along **Avenue Louise** (FS) and adjacent Avenue de la Toison d'Or, connected by the stylish **Galerie Louise** shopping centre, Boulevard de Waterloo and Porte de Namur. There are plenty of cafés and restaurants in the area for refreshment.

Marolles District (ES)

This working-class district with a tendency for rebellion has come under pressure in recent years from wealthier areas around it, in particular from the Sablon, where some businesses need space for expansion and are encroaching over the boundary. For centuries the Marolles was oppressed by the gentry, and during the late 19C the city authorities demolished a big piece of the district and set down on it the lowering bulk of the Justice Palace (*see* p.61).

There are no great monuments in the Marolles. The main reason for coming here is to see a part of the city that, though poor in economic terms, has more spirit and sense of community than wealthier areas, and seems to want nothing to do with the Euro-city vision that forces the pace and shape of change elsewhere.

A good place to enter the Marolles is near **Tour Anneessens**, a tower of the medieval fortified wall south-west of Gare Centrale in Boulevard de l'Empereur. Take Rue Haute, the longest and oldest street in the district, passing on the right a building decorated with the Hergé comic strip *Quick and Flupke*. Further along, the **Église Notre-Dame-de-la-Chapelle*** (Church of Our Lady of the Chapel) (JZ), named after a 12C chapel that developed over centuries into the present church, which features a medley of architectural styles. Inside is a **memorial** by Jan Bruegel to his father, Pieter Bruegel the Elder (c1525-69), who was married in the church.

Continue along Rue Haute, which is lined with nondescript shops and cafés, giving way to an enclave of more stylish restaurants around Rue de l'Épée and Place Pieter Bruegel. At no 132 is the house, now an irregularly open museum, where Pieter Bruegel lived and worked.

Further along, turn right into Rue des Renards, to **Place du Jeu de Balle** (ES 139), site of the famed **Vieux Marché** (Old Market), the city's top flea market and one of its great attractions, held here every morning between 7am and 1pm. You stand an excellent chance of picking up some genuine old articles here, and a good chance of finding some valuable pieces at

Experience a slice of Brussels life in the city's top flea market, Vieux Marché, in Place du Jeu de Balle.

knockdown prices. Bargain hunters and traders retire to the busy cafés and simple eateries around the square for post-market refreshment.

Return to Rue Haute and continue to its end, passing an enclave of modest Spanish restaurants on the way. Turn right into Boulevard du Midi for a short distance, to see the **Porte de Hal***, the last surviving gateway in the demolished medieval city wall (currently closed for restoration).

EUROPEAN DISTRICT (GS)

It's less a matter of Brussels being in the heart of Europe, than of Europe being at the heart of Brussels. Although it can be interesting to view the European Union's administrative and political centre – seat of the **European Commission**, **Parliament**, **Council of Ministers** and related institutions – you may find 1.2 million m^2 (12.7 million sq ft) of monumental governmental edifices, filled with 20 000-plus Eurocrats, to have a limited appeal. Many Bruxellois are indignant that characterful neighbourhoods were swept away to make space for these buildings. Notable sights remain, though, and plenty of restaurants, cafés and pubs from all corners of Europe and beyond lend animation to the scene.

Probably the best known European building is the X-shaped **Centre de Berlaymont** (GR), formerly the European Commission's headquarters, at Rond-Point Schuman. It used to make a brave display, with its European Union national flags flapping on poles beside Rue de la Loi. Identified an asbestos-laced health hazard during the early 1990s, it is now empty and hidden behind white protective sheeting while long-term renovation goes ahead.

On the opposite side of Rue de la Loi, you arrive in Euroland proper. You come first to the Art Deco **Résidence Palace** (1923-26), a former luxury apartment block that has been taken over by EU offices. Further uphill is the **Consilium**, the colossal Council of Ministers building, with its peach-coloured granite façade. Circle around this building and cross over into **Parc Léopold**, a green haven with a small lake in the midst of all the Euro-bustle. It hosts a cluster of educational institutes dating from the 1890s to the 1930s, among them the magnificent **Bibliothèque Solvay** (Solvay Library) of the Sociology Institute, with a soaring ceiling framed by wrought-iron arches and rich mahogany wainscotting.

This brings you to the curvaceous new **European Parliament**, resplendent in oceans of white marble and tinted glass. Continue through a passage in the middle of the building, fighting a powerful air current, and you come out into an old-fashioned square, Place Léopold, which has so far retained its character despite heavy pressure from its new neighbours. Decrepit little **Gare du Quartier Léopold** railway station, with its circular clock, seems mimicked on an overpowering scale by the domed **International Conference Centre** behind it.

At the south end of the park, at 29 Rue Vautier, the **Musée**

The glass and marble European Parliament has been dubbed the 'cheese box' building.

des Sciences Naturelles (Institut Royal)★★ (Museum of the Natural Sciences) (GS M[26]), housed in a former convent, is a firm favourite with children. Among highlights in this active and interactive museum, are a room filled with 29 complete **iguanadon skeletons** more than 65 million years old, found in western Belgium; 18 whale skeletons; and displays of minerals, shells, the underwater environment and reptiles.

Across the road, at no 62, the **Musée Wiertz** (GS M[28]), in the former home and studio of Antoine Wiertz (1806-65), houses 160 often grisly works by this pre-Surrealist artist (closed weekends in July and August).

Le Cinquantenaire★★★

Take the metro to Mérode station and at the Porte de Tervuren take Avenue des Gaulois. A short distance down on your left, at 5 Rue des Francs, is the 1905 **Maison Cauchie★** (HS K[1]), an Art Nouveau house with diaphanous murals by architect Paul Cauchie (*see* p.81).

Begun in 1875 to celebrate the 1880 golden jubilee of Belgian independence, though many of its elements were not completed until later, this monumental complex consists of an ornamental park surrounding a triumphal arch, the **Arc du Cinquantenaire**, flanked by colonnaded pavilions and fronted by a fountain. On top of the arch is a bronze chariot group representing *Brabant Raising the National Flag*. If this were all the Cinquantenaire had to offer, it would be little more than an overstated monument to King Léopold II's grandiose vision of national glory, but the pavilions house three excellent museums. The north wing and hall house the Army

Museum, the south hall contains the Autoworld exhibition and the south wing the Musée du Cinquantenaire.

The eclectic **Musée du Cinquantenaire★★★** (HS M[11]), is among the best in the country, combining the Royal Museums of Art and History to form one of the largest collections in Europe. Its 140 rooms contain art and artefacts from around the world, representing periods ranging from the Stone Age to 19C Belgian Art Nouveau. Particularly well-represented are the Ancient civilisations: outstanding exhibits include Mesopotamian and Phoenician reliefs and figurines; Egyptian mummies and stelae; early Greek ceramics; and a scale model of ancient Rome. The America Rooms on level I include pre-Columbian and ethnographic art, stunning Mayan, Toltec and Aztec gold ornaments and Polynesian ceremonial

Symbol of Belgium's unity and national pride, the Arc du Cinquantenaire.

Admiring the stitchwork on the fine medieval tapestries, Musée du Cinquantenaire.

objects. Religious relics from India and beautiful Chinese silks are the highlights of the India, China and South East Asia section on level III. European decorative arts through the ages are well-represented too, including splendidly-coloured medieval tapestries and fine Renaissance and Baroque furniture and ornaments.

Adjacent to the Cinquantenaire Museum, **Autoworld★★** (HS M[3]) sports a gleaming collection of around 450 cars and other vintage, historical and curio vehicles. Among them are 15 Minerva cars (the Belgian Rolls-Royce), the oldest dating from 1910. In addition, the big viewing hall holds eye-catching cars from America, Britain, Germany, France, Italy and other countries.

On the other side of the arch is the **Musée Royal de l'Armée et de l'Histoire Militaire** (Royal Museum of the Army and Military History) (HS M[25]). Pieces in its wide-ranging armoury collection long predate Belgium's foundation, and include suits of armour and other weaponry from the Middle Ages and the Burgundian and Habsburg periods. From there it moves up through the Napoleonic period to the First and Second World Wars, and into modern times. The **Air and Space Collection** includes an extensive array of armoured fighting vehicles and of military and civilian aircraft.

Don't leave the Cinquantenaire without touring its **park** and landscaped gardens, which contain a number of almost hidden architectural gems. These include Victor Horta's unfinished, temple-like **Pavillon des Passions Humaines** (Pavilion of the Human Passions), surrounded by Jef Lambeaux's sculptures – it was quickly closed by the authorities who considered it immoral. In the northern corner is Brussels' **Grande Mosquée** (Grand Mosque), in the remodelled 'Panorama of Cairo' pavilion from the 1880 Exhibition.

Motor enthusiasts will delight in the prestigious collection in Autoworld.

Square Ambiorix

Named after a chief of the ancient Eburones, a Belgic tribe, who defeated two of Julius Caesar's legions near Tongeren in 54 BC, **Square Ambiorix** (GR) is the heart of a tranquil district north of the Cinquantenaire, filled with genteel, late 19C-early 20C mansions. The highly ornamented **Saint-Cyr House** (1900) at no 11, is by Victor Horta's student, Gustave Strauven. Among other Art Nouveau houses are three outstanding mansions by Victor Horta himself in Avenue Palmerston, which connects Square Ambiorix to Square Marie-Louise: the **corner house** at no 2 (1898); **Hôtel Deprez-Van de Velde** (1896) at no 3; and **Hôtel van Eetvelde*** (1895-98) at no 4, notable for its swirling wrought-iron work.

Square Marie-Louise (GR 171) has a miniature lake with fountain and artificial grottoes at its centre, overlooked by late-19C houses in a variety of styles.

THE SUBURBS

Maison d'Érasme, home of the great humanist philosopher, Erasmus.

Anderlecht

Crowds head out to this western commune to watch Brussels' soccer aces RSC Anderlecht in action. Quieter pursuits are on offer at the neat, red-brick **Maison d'Érasme**** (Erasmus House), 31 Rue du Chapitre, home of the great Dutch humanist Desiderius Erasmus (1469-1536) for five months during 1521. Restored to its 16C condition, the house is filled with period art and artefacts. You can see books by Erasmus in the library. There is a fine and varied collection of paintings, including Hieronymous Bosch's late-15C *The Adoration of the Magi.*

Erasmus was a guest of the Canons of St Peter, whose 14C-15C Gothic **Collégiale des Saints-Pierre-et-Guidon**★ (Collegiate Church of St Peter and St Guido) almost equals the city's cathedral in size and splendour. Around the corner, two houses and the courtyard of the small 17C **Béguinage**, a convent for women, now house a museum of local history, art and folklore.

From the attic to the cellar of Musée de la Gueuze, the taste of tradition is at work to provide an inimitable, slightly acid beer.

Don't leave Anderlecht without visiting the **Musée de la Gueuze**★ (ES M19) at the Cantillon Brewery in Rue Gheude. This is the city's last family brewery, producing traditional *lambic* (fermenting beer without yeast), and also *gueuze, kriek* and *faro* beers.

Bruparck

The **Parc des Expositions** (Exhibitions Park), the first important structure on the Heysel plateau, north-west of the Royal Estate, was built for the 1935 World Fair. It was extended for the 1958 World Fair and

further expanded since then. Its heart is the 1935 **Grand Palais** (Grand Palace), a grandiose exhibition hall fronted with a fountain and pools, that seems almost fascist in its inspiration.

Downhill in Boulevard du Centenaire stands the monument that most people come here to see, the **Atomium★**, an astonishing piece of engineering from 1958 that looks impressive from a distance and awesome close up. Representing the atomic structure of an iron molecule magnified 165 billion times, its nine giant metallic spheres equalled the number of Belgian provinces when it was built (a tenth province, though not a tenth sphere, has since been added).

Take a tour of Europe's great sights in an hour or so at Mini-Europe, Bruparck.

An elevator takes you up to a viewing deck (102m/335ft) that provides a magnificent outlook. You can then go down via the escalators or stairs, visiting a temporary exhibition on the way.

Bruparck, despite a certain artificiality, has become hugely popular since it opened in 1988. It groups together a number of attractions. The best of these is **Mini-Europe**, a park in which outstanding buildings and locations from the European Union's 15 member countries are reproduced on a 1:25 scale. The detail on some models – the Houses of Parliament in London, the Escorial Palace near Madrid, the Brandenburg Gate in Berlin, the Grand-Place in Brussels – is exquisite. Other models include the Channel Tunnel and an Ariane V rocket that actually 'lifts off'. Bruparck also has the **Kinepolis** 28-screen cinema multiplex; **Océade** waterpark, with slides and artificial waves; and **The Village**, a cluster of restaurants, cafés and souvenir shops in the style of a Flemish village. Also in the Heysel complex are the **Roi Baudoin** national football stadium, and a **Planetarium**.

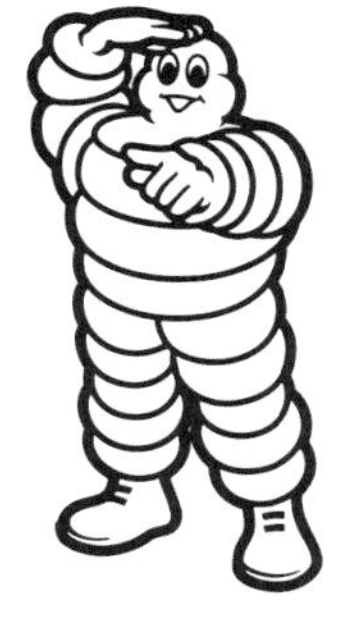

Ixelles★

Originally a village outside the walls and long since swallowed up by the city, **Ixelles★** (FST) is a multifaceted part of Brussels with fine houses, restaurants and shops, and plenty of green spaces.

You can take a walk through the green heart of Ixelles, starting at the neo-Classical **Maison Communale★** (Town Hall, 1833) (FS K[2]) in Place Fernand Cocq. Take Rue van Aa to the **Musée Communal d'Ixelles★★** (Ixelles Commune Museum) (GT M[12]), at

Rue van Volsem 71, housed partly in a former slaughterhouse. This under-appreciated museum, founded in 1892, houses works by Picasso, Magritte, Rembrandt and Rodin, among others, together with a collection of posters, including almost all the posters designed by Toulouse-Lautrec.

Go south-west along Rue Malibran to **Place Flagey**, a busy traffic intersection; on the corner stands the old **Institut National de Radiodiffusion** (INR), a studio from 1935-37 designed in the style of a passenger liner. Ahead of you are the tree-lined **Étangs d'Ixelles** (Ixelles Ponds) – small artificial lakes in the Maelbeek River valley that are a haven for ducks and are overlooked by handsome townhouses on either side.

The Abbaye de la Cambre is a peaceful enclave, where the stormy past has given way to harmonious abbey lodgings and beautiful terraced gardens.

On their west bank you pass the **Jardin du Roi** (King's Garden), established in 1873 by King Léopold II. This brings you to the delightful Cistercian **Abbaye de la Cambre★★**, founded in 1201, and its 16C Gothic church. In a turbulent history, the abbey was destroyed and rebuilt several times before being closed by the French in 1796. This idyllic setting, surrounded by gardens and pools, houses the National Geographical Institute and the National School of Architecture and Decorative Arts.

Leave by Avenue Louise and continue southwards, into **Bois de la Cambre★**, the city's biggest park. Laid out during the 1860s in the natural English style to create a country scene inside the city, the park is hugely popular, particularly in summer and at weekends. A lake in its southern part has a little island reached by electric punt; the island's characterful Chalet Robinson café-restaurant burned down some years ago and has not been rebuilt.

Jette

If you're interested in the life of Surrealist artist René Magritte, a visit to the **Musée Magritte** (Rue Esseghem 135) will be something of a pilgrimage. His home in this north-western commune, from 1930 until 1954, has been turned into a museum that gives an idea of how he lived and worked.

Koekelberg

The ambience of the red-brick **Basilique du Sacré-Coeur*** (Basilica of the Sacred Heart), one of the world's biggest churches, has lost something by being at the focus of a busy road system. Yet the visual impact of this great church remains, as does the fine **view** of Brussels from a 50m- (162ft) high circular gallery running round its immense bronze dome (*see* p.7). During the long construction period (1905-70), the heavy, neo-Gothic plan was complemented by Art Deco elements and embellished with modern stained-glass windows.

Laeken

Even more than Place Royale and the Royal Palace in central Brussels, **Laeken** is the district most closely associated with Belgium's royal family (it is best to tour by car as sights are far apart). In this area is the Royal Estate, containing the royal residence, the **Château Royale** (Royal Château). This is closed to the public, except during a few weeks in summer when you can visit the wrought-iron-and-glass **Serres Royales**★★ (Royal Greenhouses). These magnificent structures date from 1873 and were built, as was so much of the city's monumental architecture, on the orders of King Léopold II; they house a lush and steamy hotbed of flowering tropical plants and trees.

We also have Léopold II to thank for two architectural curiosities at the north end of the estate (both open to the public). The **Pavillon Chinois** (Chinese Pavilion,

The bronze dome of the massive Basilique du Sacré-Coeur is one of the city's great viewpoints.

1901-09), built partly by Shanghai craftsmen, houses a collection of fine Chinese and Japanese porcelain. The **Tour Japonaise** (Japanese Tower, 1901-04) is a replica Buddhist pagoda, also built in part by native craftsmen, and houses Oriental exhibitions. The internal decoration includes some outstanding French stained-glass windows on the grand staircase.

Beside these exotic structures, the **Parc de Laeken** (Laeken Park) is a wooded, rolling area (mostly open to the public) with ornamental gardens, in which stands the **Villa Belvédère**, King Albert II's preferred

The incongruous Chinese Pavilion, in Laeken's Royal Estate.

residence, and the **Château du Stuyvenberg**, a residence for distinguished foreign guests.

Just outside the Royal Estate, to the south-west, stands the neo-Gothic **Église Notre-Dame de Laeken** (Church of Our Lady of Laeken), containing the **royal crypt**, the final resting place of Kings Léopold I, II and

A sombre memorial to the nation's royalty, in the Royal crypt, Église Notre-Dame de Laeken.

III, King Albert I, and King Baudouin I, as well as queens, princes and princesses. Many well-known Belgians, among them architect Joseph Poelaert, are buried in the adjacent **Cimitière de Laeken** (Laeken Cemetery).

Saint-Gilles

You hear a lot about Art Nouveau architecture in Brussels (*see* p.80). Whenever the style is discussed it is invariably linked with its most famous practitioner, Victor Horta (1861-1947). At the **Musée Horta**★★ (23-25 Rue Américaine) you can see how the master responded to the freedom of designing his own home and studio. Surprisingly, the exterior of the two side-by-side houses is plain, at least in comparison with other Art Nouveau façades in the city. On the inside, however, Horta gave free rein to his characteristic swirling curves and naturalistic images, using glass, iron and wood. Every item of furnishing and decor, down to the tiniest details, complements the overall effect.

Round off your visit to Saint-Gilles with a drive or walk around the streets, where many of the private houses are fine examples of Art Nouveau design, often embellished with typical architectural details and *sgraffiti*.

Woluwe-Saint-Pierre

Going eastwards out of town, along tree-lined Avenue de Tervuren, brings you to three sights in quick succession. The first is **Palais Stoclet***, at nos 279-281, a sparely designed private mansion built between 1905 and 1911, and an early work of modernism that stands in stark contrast to the contemporaneous, ornate Art Nouveau works for which Brussels is renowned. You can view it only from the outside.

Pass the **Parc de Woluwe**, with its boating ponds, on the way to the **Musée du Transport Urbain Bruxellois** (Brussels City Transport Museum), at Avenue de Tervuren 364b. At weekends and on public holidays you can ride one of the museum's superb collection of vintage trams to the **Royal Museum of Central Africa**** (*see* p. 85).

Palais Stoclet is widely acknowledged as a key example of 20C modernism.

Art Nouveau

As if it was not enough for Brussels to be capital of Europe, Belgium and Flanders, it also lays fair claim to being capital of Art Nouveau. No other city boasts such a legacy from this progressive, turn-of-the-century movement in architecture and design, which sought to escape from bourgeois, neo-Classical restrictions. Being able to point to works by, among others, architects **Paul Hankar**, **Henry van de Velde**, **Ernest Blérot, Gustave Strauven**, **Paul Cauchie**, and above all **Victor Horta**, supports this assertion.

The city's first, faint taste of the new wave appeared in elements of Horta's 1889 **pavilion** in Parc du Cinquantenaire to house *The Human Passions* sculptures by Jef Lambeaux. Among Horta's great works, in which he characteristically integrates exterior and interior design, furnishings and fittings, are three private houses: **Hôtel Tassel** (6 Rue Paul-Émile Janson), **Hôtel Solvay** (224 Avenue Louise), and **Hôtel van Eetvelde*** (4 Avenue Palmerston).

Horta's buildings, though distinctive on the outside, preserved enough sobriety to fit in smoothly with their sedate neighbours. Inside, he allowed his imagination full rein. Nowhere will you see Art Nouveau's swirling, sinuous shapes, often based on natural forms but incorporating modern materials such as iron, to better advantage than in the house he designed for himself in 1893, at 23-25 Rue Américaine, now the **Horta Museum**★★.

Other architects, inspired by Horta, added their own distinctive inspiration to the genre, some imitated, and yet others produced pastiches – it's interesting to choose between these various interpretations as you tour Brussels' Art Nouveau legacy. Look out for additional masterpieces such as the extravagant **Maison de Saint-Cyr** (11 Square Ambiorix, 1903) by 22-year-old Gustave Strauven, and the astonishing **Maison Cauchie**★ (5 Rue des Francs, 1905), replete with *sgraffito* murals, by Paul Cauchie.

You can enjoy a drink or a meal in Art Nouveau surroundings at **Le Falstaff**, 17-19 Rue Henri Maus, and **De Ultieme Hallucinatie**, 316 Rue Royale.

Left: Musée Horta.

Right: Maison Cauchie.

Uccle

Come to this southern commune to visit the **Musée David et Alice van Buuren★** (Avenue Léo Errera 41), an Art Deco house that displays an eclectic collection of art and other objects collected by the Van Buuren family. These include Pieter Bruegel's *The Fall of Icarus*. The charming gardens offer a refreshing change, or you can wander in the circular park surrounding the **Observatoire Royal** (Royal Observatory), near Saint-Job railway station.

The jewel of art amateurs, the Musée David et Alice van Buuren with its Art Deco interior is set in splendid gardens.

Watermael-Boitsfort

The garden-in-the-city image of this commune is enhanced by the **Parc Tournay-Solvay** in its southern reaches, adjoining the **Forêt de Soignes**★★ (Soignes Forest). The dense forest, a remnant of the great forest that covered much of Belgium in ancient times, and a popular place for a weekend stroll, stretches south-eastwards beyond Brussels Capital Region, across a strip of Flanders, into Wallonia, reaching almost as far as Waterloo.

Thousands gather on the Lion Mound, Waterloo, to watch a re-enactment of the famous battle.

OUTSIDE BRUSSELS

Waterloo★

If you ignore the major exception of the R0 Brussels Ring Road, which slices through its western flank, the Waterloo battlefield has not changed greatly since 18 June, 1815. On that day, combined armies of British, Germans, Dutch and Belgians, led by the Duke of Wellington and Marshal Blücher, decisively defeated the French Emperor Napoleon Bonaparte, bringing the Napeoleonic era to an end.

The Battle of Waterloo was fought 2km (1.2 miles) south-west of Waterloo, on rolling farmland around the gentle heights of Mont-Saint-Jean, on which Wellington's army was deployed to block the Brussels road. Napoleon chose to make a frontal attack on Wellington's position and persisted throughout the day, despite terrible losses, coming close to breaking the line but never quite managing it. As evening approached, Blücher's Prussians arrived from the east and attacked the French, forcing them back.

Napoleon launched a final assault with his Imperial Guard. When it was repulsed, the combined Allied armies advanced and swept the French from the field, leaving 49 000 dead and wounded.

Start your tour at the **Centre du Visiteur** (Visitor Centre), 252-254 Route du Lion. The vivid audio-visual performance explains the action on that fateful day, and from the centre you have access to the 40.5m (132ft) **Butte du Lion** (Lion Mound), raised after the battle in honour of Holland's Prince of Orange. At the foot of the mound is the **Panorama de la Bataille** (Panorama of the Battle), a circular painting 110m (358ft) in circumference, depicting the full-blooded French cavalry charge led by Marshal Ney (*see* p.15). Across the road is the **Musée des Cire** (Waxworks Museum), with wax images of the main figures on both sides.

In the town of Waterloo, visit the **Musée Wellington** (Wellington Museum), 147 Chaussée de Bruxelles, housed in a former coaching inn which was Wellington's headquarters and containing paintings, documents, weapons and memorabilia.

Rixensart

Not far from Waterloo, to the east, is **Lac de Genval** (Genval Lake), a beautiful artificial lake with a high fountain, the **Genvaloise**. The lake covers 18ha (44 acres), and you can easily walk around its shore in an hour or so to see the superb villas and pavilions dating from the early part of the century, such as the **Rendez-vous d'Amour**, based on a pavilion at Versailles. The most impressive is the Tudor-style **Château du Lac**, a luxury hotel with an excellent restaurant, which serves mineral water from four nearby springs. On a street off the lake, the **Musée de l'Eau et de la Fontaine** (Water and

Fountain Museum, 63 Avenue Hoover) has a collection of drinking fountains and displays on water distribution and quality.

Tervuren*

Cross into Flanders to visit the palatial **Koninklijk Museum voor Midden-Afrika/ Musée Royal de l'Afrique Centrale**** (Royal Museum of Central Africa). Once again, we have that indefatigable builder, King Léopold II, to thank for an attraction whose appeal has survived into modern times. Built between 1904 and 1910 to celebrate Belgium's colonial empire in the Congo, the neo-Classical museum has transcended those roots. It now goes beyond the original fascination with 'primitive' Africa to embrace many aspects of life, culture and environment in tropical countries. The surrounding estate has fine ornamental gardens with ponds and fountains.

The Musée Royal de l'Afrique Centrale, Tervuren, offers an extensive insight into African culture.

Experience Belgium's medieval past at Kasteel Beersel, near Huizingen (above), or at Kasteel Gaasbeek, near Lennik (below).

Two Castles

South-west of Brussels, **Kasteel Gaasbeek/ Château de Gaasbeek★★** (Gaasbeek Castle), near Lennik, and **Kasteel Beersel/Château de Beersel** (Beersel Castle), near Huizingen, provide a taste of medieval splendour. Turreted and moated 14C Beersel is Brabant's best preserved fortress, although the central buildings have disappeared. Gaasbeek, by contrast, has been transformed into an elegant country mansion, with gardens and rich interior decor and furnishings.

Meise

North of the city, the **Nationale Plantentuin/Jardin Botanique National★★** (National Botanical Garden) at Meise occupies a magnificent estate, with a castle, lakes, colourful plants – both outdoors and in greenhouses – and a wealth of tree

Right: Giant lily pads punctuate the pools at the Jardin Botanique National.

species. Often busy at weekends, the gardens are generally quiet during the week. Part of Meise's charm is to pretend you're strolling through your own country estate – even if you do have to keep off the grass.

You won't be able to resist a taste of the famous Grimbergen beer after finding out about it in the museum.

Grimbergen

Adjoining Meise, this village has a beautiful cobbled main square lined with 18C houses, beside the **Abdij van Grimbergen/Abbaye de Grimbergen** (Grimbergen Abbey), which was founded in the 12C but dates mostly from the 17C. The interior, with its majestic dome and soaring vaulted ceilings, is adorned with ornate Baroque decorations. Look out for the allegories and figures carved on the **confessionals★**. The abbey has a garden café where you can taste Trappist Grimbergen beer.

EXCURSIONS FROM BRUSSELS

Mechelen and Leuven are accessible by train or bus, but you will need a car for the other two excursions.

Mechelen★★ (Malines)

This tranquil, historic Flemish town lies along the River Dijle some 22km (14 miles) north of Brussels and is an important religious centre, being the seat of the Catholic Primate of Belgium. Although its recorded history stretches back to before Roman times, its golden age was during the Burgundian and early Habsburg periods. Charles the Bold established his Grand Council (Parliament) here in 1473. Mechelen was the favourite town of Margaret of Austria, aunt of Emperor Charles V. During her regency (1506-15) she governed the Low Countries from Mechelen and developed a brilliant court culture by inviting prominent artists, philosophers – among them Erasmus – and musicians.

Start your tour in the **Grote Markt***, which has a statue of Margaret of Austria in the middle and fine buildings around the edge, including the 14C Gothic **Lakenhalle** (Cloth Hall) and 16C Late-Gothic **Paleis van de Grote Raad** (Palace of the Grand Council), now the **Stadhuis*** (Town Hall) – the

An elegant trio – the 16C Late-Gothic Grand Council Building, and 14C belfry and former cloth hall now comprise Mechelen Stadhuis.

building was not completed until the early 20C, using the original 16C plans by architect Rombout Keldermans.

The undoubted highlight of the main square is **Sint-Romboutskathedraal**★★ (St Rombold's Cathedral), begun in the 13C and completed in the 16C. Among the cathedral's artistic treasures is the painting *The Crucifixion* by Anthony van Dyck. The 97m (315ft) belfry, which houses two 49-bell carillons and a third with seven bells which ring out every day at noon, has a shaved-off look because it was originally intended to reach 167m (543ft) but construction was abandoned in the 1520s.

Mechelen has been noted since medieval times for carillons, tapestry and lace – it houses the world-renowned **Koninklijke**

The Grote Markt, Mechelen, with St Rombold's Cathedral behind.

One of the 105 bells in St Rombold's tower.

Beiaardschool (Royal Carillon School) and is known as 'the city of bells'. In a 15C former abbey, at Schoutestraat 7, the country's last big tapestry maker, the **Koninklijke Manufactuur van Wandtapijten*** (Royal Tapestry Manufacturers), makes modern tapestries and repairs old ones. Conducted tours take you through the workshops, where the traditional skills of hand-made tapestry work are still practised. The **Hof van Busleyden Museum** (65 Frederik van Merodestraat) is the city museum, housed in an aristocratic mansion dating from 1503-08. It includes paintings, tapestries, sculptures and furnishings from medieval to modern times, and incorporates the **Beiaardmuseum** (Carillon Museum).

Margaret of Austria's early-16C palace, now the **Justitiepaleis** (Justice Palace), in Keizerstraat, was begun in the Late Gothic style and finished in the newly fashionable Renaissance style.

If you are travelling with children, take them to the **Speelgoed Museum** (Toy Museum), at Nekkerspoelstraat 21, to see all kinds of traditional and modern toys, board games and puzzles.

Leuven** (Louvain)

Leuven preceded Brussels in time and importance, for the 10C Counts of Louvain were instrumental in founding Brussels, and the town was the original seat of the Duchy of Brabant. Although Brussels is now much more important, the Flemish town 24km (16 miles) to its east retains the edge academically, thanks to the highly regarded **Katholiek Universiteit Leuven** (Leuven Catholic University), Belgium's oldest university, founded in 1425, and which has 25 000 students.

Arriving at Leuven railway station, take Bondgenotenlaan and follow it straight to the **Grote Markt**. Here stands the **Stadhuis***** (Town Hall), an intricate work of Gothic architecture that vies with Bruges' for the honour of being Belgium's most handsome town hall. Built between 1439 and 1469 along the lines of a religious reliquary, it has so many gables, turrets, pinnacles and statues in niches that it is hard to take in all at once.

Attractive gabled buildings surround Leuven's Grote Markt.

Across the square, which is lined with cafés, stands the **Sint-Pieterskerk*** (Church of St Peter), a Brabant Gothic edifice in white sandstone begun in about 1410, and never quite completed. Inside, a lavishly Baroque altar competes with the dignified simplicity of the Gothic lines. The church's treasury houses remarkable works of art in its **Museum voor Religieuze Kunst**** (Museum of Religious Art). Most notable is the **Last Supper****, masterpiece of Dirk Bouts, the renowned 15C Primitive painter who made his home in Leuven.

If you have time, take Mechelsestraat in the direction of the huge Stella Artois brewery, for a look at what remains of the 13C **Klein Begijnhof** (Small Beguinage) and the facing 14C **Sint-Gertrudiskerk** (Church of St Gertrude), with its grand spire.

Otherwise go south through **Oude Markt**, a busy square with many cafés and restaurants which are popular with students, then take Parijsstraat and Schapenstraat to the **Groot Begijnhof**★★ (Grand Beguinage). Founded in about 1230, this community for pious religious women – not nuns – is Belgium's biggest beguinage. Though now transformed into student accommodation, it seems like an island of the Middle Ages and Renaissance in the heart of town, and you can stroll around the courtyard and cobbled alleys.

Return to the station via Namsestraat and Vlamingstraat passing, on Herbert Hooverplein, the **Universiteitsbibliotheek** (University Library), a post-First World War reconstruction of a 15C library that was destroyed in 1914.

The Stadhuis and Grote Markt take on a theatrical air when floodlit at night.

Abbaye de Villers-la-Ville**

The ruins of the once powerful Cistercian Abbey of Villers-la-Ville, which was founded in 1147 by St Bernard of Clairvaux, are among the most striking sights in Belgium. Incorporating Romanesque, Gothic and Renaissance elements, they represent all the architectural styles that flourished in Brabant from the 12C to the 18C. The cloister's great size alone – it housed 300 monks in the 13C – would make this an interesting scene but the mouldering ruins have a romantic aspect that adds greatly to the experience.

Over such a long period, the abbey's fortunes inevitably waxed and waned. It was sacked by both Protestant rebels and pro-Catholic Spanish during the 16C, and by Austrian and French troops at the end of the 18C. You can visit the remains of the abbot's palace, cloisters, monks' quarters, chapter house, church – which collapsed in 1884 – and the brewery.

The wonderful abbey ruins at Villers-la-Ville are the largest in Belgium.

Château de Seneffe**

This magnificent neo-Classical château, set in a 22ha (54 acres) park, was built between 1763 and 1768 as the summer residence of Count Julien Depestre. Designed by architect Laurent-Benoît Dewez, the blue-stone chateau is at the centre of a remarkable group of buildings, which includes an orangery, a small neo-Classical theatre, an icehouse and extensive gardens. As a bonus, Seneffe houses the **Musée de l'Orfèvrerie** (Silverware Museum), incorporating the European silver collection of Claude and Juliette d'Allemagne.

Owned throughout most of its history by individuals who added to its allure and preserved its original spirit, Seneffe fell on hard times from the 1950s until 1970, when the state acquired it and began a 25-year campaign of consolidation and repair that has restored the château almost to its original splendour.

You enter the estate along a 600m (656yd), tree-lined driveway from the church in Seneffe village, 50km (31 miles) south of Brussels. The two-storey main building, fronted by three groups of Corinthian columns, is flanked by two long open galleries, lined with Ionic columns each ending in a domed pavilion. Inside, the public and private suites form a lavish ensemble of stuccoed ceilings, mirrors, paintings, and superb period furniture and fittings. In addition to the silverware collections, of special note are the floors, made of precious woods. You can also stroll in the gardens, which are being restored at present.

WEATHER

In a country described by its great singer/songwriter, Jacques Brel (1929-78), as having 'a sky so low that it engenders humility; a sky so grey that it has to be forgiven for it', you can guess that grey skies and rain are a significant part of the weather pattern. Fortunately, they are not the only part, although rain can be expected in any month.

April, May and early June are the spring months – generally mild but with showers and cold snaps always a possibility. September and October present a similar picture for autumn, with temperatures dropping down and the amount of rain increasing as the season rolls by. Winter runs from November to March, with temperatures sliding to a trough that rarely reaches more than a few degrees below zero. Rain, sometimes freezing rain, is always a threat but there are plenty of cold but sunny days, with blue skies. Snow is not a regular occurrence – indeed, the occasional fall brings people to Grand-Place to enjoy the romantic scene it creates.

Summer, in terms of sunshine, really means July and August, and, if you're lucky, a sliver of June and September. In all but exceptional years you can count on consistent warm sunshine, with temperatures generally in the mid-20s, reaching into the 30s during heatwaves, punctuated by an occasional humdinger of a thunderstorm that cools things down sharply.

CALENDAR OF EVENTS

There are a great many events held in Brussels, a few of which are regular events that attract great interest.

January: *Antiques Fair* (in Palais des Beaux-Arts) and *Brussels International Film Festival* (Porte de Namur) generally take place towards the end of the month.

May: *Queen Elisabeth International Music Competition* for young musicians (continues into June). *Brussels Jazz Marathon* takes place during the last weekend in May.

June: Carillon Concerts begin at St Rombold's Cathedral, Mechelen, and continue until the end of August. *Couleur Café*, a world music event, is held at Tour et Taxis, Rue Picard, Molenbeek-St-Jean at the end of June.

July: On the first Tuesday and Thursday of the month, the *Ommegang* procession in Grand-Place re-creates the pageantry with which, in 1549, Brussels welcomed Emperor Charles V. Grand-Place is also a stage for concerts, theatre, dance and other entertainment. The *Brosella Ferdurfolk Jazz Festival,* in the second weekend, is held in Heysel. Brussels celebrates *Belgian National Day* with parades and music in front of the Royal Palace.

August: *Planting of the May Tree* ceremony is held in the City Centre. Every second (even-numbered) year, Grand-Place is the setting for the *Carpet of Flowers,* a giant tapestry 'woven' from begonias. *Marktrock* brings two-days of rock and jazz to Leuven's Grote Markt.

3 September: On *Liberation Day,* Manneken Pis dons the uniform of the Welsh Guards to celebrate the liberation of Brussels by Allied troops in 1944.

December: The *Christmas Market* runs throughout the month in Grand-Place, accompanied by a Nativity Scene with real animals, and a Christmas Tree.

The Carpet of Flowers, Grand-Place.

ACCOMMODATION

Although Brussels has **hotels** in all its communes, there are important concentrations in the Lower City, around Grand-Place and Place Sainte-Catherine; the Upper City, along Rue Royale and Avenue Louise and adjoining streets; Place Rogier, near the Gare du Nord; and the European District.

The city has overcapacity in hotel beds, because big hotel chains want to be represented in the 'Capital of Europe', even though there is generally not enough business to go around. Room rates vary greatly as, at all but the busiest times of the year, there is a considerable number of unsold rooms. This has two main effects: higher grade hotels often drop their prices to rates one or two grades below what they would normally charge, in turn squeezing the rates of lower grade hotels; most hotels are willing to offer better rates than their official ones – if you ask.

Hotels are graded from one to five stars, with rates and standards increasing to levels that come close to matching the highest in the world. Below the one-star level there are 'O' and 'H' grade hotels, representing very basic levels of facilities and service. Rooms can be booked through **Belgium Tourist Reservations**, Boulevard Anspach 111, 1000 Brussels ☎ **02 513 74 84** Fax 02 513 92 77; **OPT**, 61 Rue du Marché-aux-Herbes, 1000 Brussels ☎ **02 504 03 90** Fax 02 504 02 70; or through the **Office de Tourisme et d'Information de Bruxelles (TIB)**, Grand-Place, 1000 Brussels ☎ **02 513 89 40** Fax 02 514 45 38. A brochure listing accommodation in Brussels can be obtained from **Tourism Flanders-Brussels**, 31 Pepper Street, London E14 9RW ☎ **0891 88 77 99**.

The following prices are a guide to what you can expect to pay for a double room, per night, with breakfast:

5 star: over 10 000 BF
4 star: 5 000-10 000 BF
3 star: 3 000-5 000 BF
2 star: 2 000-3 000 BF
1 star: under 2 000 BF

The Michelin *Red Guide Benelux* lists accommodation and restaurants in Brussels and the surrounding area, and is revised annually.

Bed and breakfast provides reasonably priced accommodation. For a brochure or to make reservations, contact **Bed & Brussels**, 2 Rue Gustave Biot, 1050 Brussels ☎ **02 646 07 37** Fax 02 644 01 14; **Taxistop**, 28 Rue du Fossé-aux-Loups, 1000 Brussels ☎ **02 223 22 31** Fax 02

223 22 32; or the **TIB**, Grand-Place, 1000 Brussels ☎ **02 513 89 40** Fax 02 514 45 38.

For details of **youth hostels** and other accommodation for young people and students, contact **Les Auberges de la Jeunesse de Wallonie**, 52 Rue Van Oost, 1030 Brussels; ☎ **02 215 31 00** or **Vlaamse Jeugdherberg-Centrale**, 40 Van Stralenstraat, 2060 Antwerp; ☎ **03 232 72 18**. There are five youth hostels in Brussels:

Auberge de Jeunesse Jacques Brel, 30 Rue de la Sablonnière, 1000 Brussels ☎ **02 218 01 87** Fax 02 217 20 05

Auberge de Jeunesse de la Fonderie Jean Nihon, 4 Rue de l'Eléphant, 1080 Brussels ☎ **02 410 38 58** Fax 02 410 35 05

Jeugdherberg Bruegel IYHF, Rue Saint-Ésprit, 1000 Brussels ☎ **02 511 04 36** Fax 02 512 07 11

Hôtel de Jeunes Sleep Well, Espace du Marais, 23 Rue du Damier, 1000 Brussels ☎ **02 218 50 50** Fax 02 218 13 13

Centre Vincent Van Gough, CHAB, 8 Rue Traversière ☎ **02 217 01 58** Fax 02 219 79 95.

Attractive wooden houses line the wharfs, Mechelen.

Recommendations

Lower City

Radisson SAS *47 Rue du Fossé-aux-Loups, 1000 Brussels* ☎ **02 219 28 28** Fax 02 219 62 62
Modern and stylish – even though it incorporates part of the old city wall. Rooms are decorated in a variety of national styles from around the world. (12 000-15 000 BF)

Royal Windsor *5 Rue Duquesnoy, 1000 Brussels* ☎ **02 505 55 55**
Fax 02 505 55 00
Modern hotel with a full range of facilities and a perfect location in the town centre. (12 000 BF)

Astoria *103 Rue Royale, 1000 Brussels* ☎ **02 227 05 05**
Fax 02 217 11 50
A *belle époque* beauty, that combines plush elegance with modern comforts, in a memorable setting. (5 000-13 000 BF)

Métropole *31 Place de Brouckère, 1000 Brussels* ☎ **02 217 23 00**
Fax 02 218 02 20
A taste of old-fashioned class in an elegant turn-of-the-century hotel which has been renovated to modern standards. (10 500-12 500 BF)

Le Dix-Septième *25 Rue de la Madeleine, 1000 Brussels* ☎ **02 502 57 44** Fax 02 502 64 24
More like an 18C stately home than a hotel, thanks to lavish amounts of wood panelling and marble. Close to Grand-Place. (6 000-7 000 BF)

Art Hotel Siru *1 Place Rogier, 1210 Brussels* ☎ **02 203 35 80**
Fax 02 203 33 03
Each room in this chic hotel has been 'decorated' by a modern Belgian artist with a work of art on the theme of travel. (5 500-6 000 BF)

Albert Premier *20 Place Rogier, 1210 Brussels* ☎ **02 203 31 25**
Fax 02 203 43 31
Behind its graceful 19C façade, this hotel, which at one stage seemed to have fallen on hard times, has been refurbished to bring it up to modern standards. (3 000-4 500 BF)

Mozart *23 Rue du Marché-aux-Fromages, 1000 Brussels* ☎ **02 502 66 61** Fax 02 502 77 58
A great location around the corner from Grand-Place; straight-forward furnishings in rooms with half-timbered ceilings (avoid the rooms facing the street, which can be noisy). (2 500-4 000 BF)

Welcome *5 Rue du Peuplier, 1000 Brussels* ☎ **02 219 95 46**
Fax 02 217 18 87
Count yourself fortunate to be staying here, as the hotel only has six rooms; if you are lucky, though, you'll appreciate its blend of friendly, personal service. (2 300-3 200 BF)

Pacific *57 Rue Antoine Dansaert, 1000 Brussels* ☎/Fax **02 511 84 59**

Small, characterful hotel run by an enthusiastic owner, which adds value beyond its fairly simple facilities.
(1 000-1 750 BF)

Upper City

Hôtel-Résidence Albert *27-29 Rue Royale-Sainte-Marie, 1030 Brussels* ☎ **02 217 93 91**
Fax 02 219 20 17
Modern comforts for a reasonable price in a location that verges on being off the beaten track, though with good connections to the centre.
(1 800-2 500 BF)

Les Bluets *124 Rue Berckmans, 1060 Brussels* ☎ **02 534 39 83**
Fax 02 543 09 70
Rambling, cluttered with antiques and bric-a-brac, and loaded with charm, this marvellous old place treats you like a guest in a family home.
(1 650-2 450 BF)

Mouthwatering seafood display.

FOOD AND DRINK

It is for good reason that 'Burgundian' and 'Bruegelian' are commonly heard epithets for Brussels – indeed for Belgium as a whole. The expressions find their origins in the lavish feasts given by the Dukes of Burgundy at their Brussels court during the 15C and 16C, and in paintings by Pieter Bruegel of peasants tucking into holiday feasts, with tables groaning under their burden of food and drink. You'll be hard put to eat badly in Brussels, whatever price you elect to pay.

Main Dishes

Belgian cuisine is regional cuisine, although by now most dishes have crossed the linguistic and cultural barrier between Flanders and Wallonia and can be found in both, as well as being adapted to modern tastes by chefs who like to experiment with the basic ingredients and come up with new variations on old favourites.

Moules et frites (mussels and fries) is the national dish – even though the mussels, cooked in steaming pots of vegetable stock or white wine, come from Zeeland in Holland, and the provenance of 'French' fries has been so badly misconstrued. *L'américain*, or *steak-frites* (steak and chips), is a close competitor to the mussels from Brussels.

A Brussels tradition is cooking with local beers to produce dishes such as *lapin à la gueuze* (rabbit in *gueuze* sauce). Look also for popular Flemish dishes, such as *water-zooï op Gentse wijze* (fish or chicken stew from Ghent) and *paling in 't groen* (eel in a green sauce). Specialities from Wallonia include smoked *jambon d'Ardenne* (Ardennes ham); *salade liégeoise,* a mixture of smoked bacon, potatoes, onion, parsley and French beans; and *ragoût liégois,* a stew of potatoes, vegetables and veal and, during the autumn game season, wild boar, venison, hare and wildfowl.

The coast supplies delicacies such as *maatjes,* filleted and lightly salted raw herring, usually served with raw onions; sole, in particular served as *sole à l'Ostendaise*; and grey North Sea shrimps, some of which are caught at Oostduinkerke by fishermen riding sturdy horses into the waves – try them as *tomates aux crevettes* (tomato stuffed with shrimp and mayon-naise) and *croquettes de crevettes* (deep-fried shrimp cakes). Try also *écrevisses à la liégeoise* (crayfish in a butter, cream, and white wine sauce).

For vegetables, try *asperges* (asparagus), often as *asperges à la Flamande,* white asparagus served with sliced or crumbled egg and melted butter; *chicon* (chicory/Belgian endive), often served wrapped in slices of ham with cheese sauce; and, of course, Brussels sprouts. *Stoemp,* mashed potatoes and vegetables, is a good standby, though not for vegetarians as it is generally accompanied by sausage or other meat.

Snacks

You can buy *gaufres* – Belgian waffles topped with sugar, plain or caramelised; filled with fruit or whipped cream; and covered in chocolate. The traditional Maison J Dandoy, at 14-18 Rue Charles Buls, near Grand-Place, sells very good ones. There is also a range of special Belgian biscuits (*spéculo, cramiques* and so on) which you can buy to take away or eat in the tea rooms. *Frites,* accompanied by mayonnaise, tomato ketchup, or some other sauce, and fried twice to seal in their flavour, are sold at numerous street stalls.

Cheese

Belgium produces a great range of **cheeses**, many of them gems of small-scale production, and some of which are produced by monks. Among the more than 300 varieties, try brands such as

Château d'Arville, Corsendonck, Maredsous, Passendale, Petrus, Le Regalou, Rubens and Wynendale.

Chocolates

Handmade **pralines** by Belgian companies such as Wittamer, Nihoul, Neuhaus, Godiva, and Leonidas, and by individual shops such as Chocolatier Mary, 73 Rue Royale, and Chocolatier Marcolini, 39 Place du Grand Sablon, can be found all over the city. Pralines in boxes weighing from 100g up to 2kg and more make great presents, and the chocolates are also good to eat on the spot. Many are made with fresh cream, so you shouldn't keep them for long – as if you would. Buy them in ready-made selections or make your own choice by pointing to the ones you want.

Drinks

Belgium produces some 400 brands of **beer** (*see* p.105), and it's perfectly acceptable to drink beer with a meal rather than wine (all wine is imported).

As a *digestif*, or on its own in a café, try a *genièvre* (*jenever* in Dutch), a potent grain-spirit. Belgium has 70 *genièvre* distilleries which produce some 270 brands, such as Filliers Oude Graanjenever, De Poldenaar Oude Antwerpsche, Heinrich Pèkèt de la Piconette, Sint-Pol, and Van Damme. Some are flavoured with juniper, coriander, and other herbs and spices.

Belgian chocolates.

Where to Eat

You can make a good case for saying there are no bad districts for eating in this food-gastronomic city, but a few areas stand out as having more good restaurants per square metre than others, and often the restaurants have outdoor tables. The most popular district, and the easiest to find as it's around Grand-Place, is the **Îlot Sacré**, and in particular Rue des Bouchers, Petite Rue des Bouchers and adjacent sidestreets. They present a veritable United Nations of cuisine styles. Although not all Belgian restaurants in this area come up to scratch, some are very good.

For seafood, you can't do better than the **Marché-aux-Poissons**; the Fish Market has a number of top-flight restaurants and an atmospheric location, in particular when the weather is good and the pavement terraces are in service. Other districts in the city centre with many restaurants are: **Place du Grand-Sablon** and the streets downhill from it, and also the area around **Place Saint-Géry**, which includes Chinatown.

In the Upper City, head for **Place Stéphanie**, **Avenue Louise** and **Porte de Namur** where there is a cluster of good places. **Ixelles** commune has a great many fine restaurants scattered through its streets.

Ethnic enclaves include Chinese and Vietnamese restaurants in **Boulevard Anspach** opposite the Bourse; Indian and Pakistani on **Chaussée de Louvain**; Turkish along **Chaussée de Haecht**; and Spanish and Portuguese in **Rue Haute**.

Below are a few restaurants and cafés, which capture the Burgundian spirit of eating and drinking in Brussels. The restaurants are all in the moderate and budget price range, except where otherwise indicated, and serve Belgian specialities or a mixture of Belgian and French cuisine in attractive and interesting settings.

Recommendations

Restaurants

Grand-Place and Îlot Sacré

La Maison du Cygne *2 Rue Charles Buls* ☎ **02 511 82 44** Formal French dining in a superb setting overlooking Grand-Place. Expensive.

Aux Armes de Bruxelles *13 Rue des Bouchers* ☎ **02 511 55 98** One of the Îlot Sacré's most consistent performers (try the shrimp croquettes).

De l'Ogenblik *1 Galerie des Princes* ☎ **02 511 61 51** Chic bistro in the elegant Galeries Saint-Hubert shopping arcade. Moderate to expensive.

La Roue d'Or *26 Rue des Chapeliers* ☎ **02 514 25 54** Cheerful place with Magritte images on the walls and wholehearted Belgian food on the plates.

't Kelderke *15 Grand-Place* ☎ **02 513 73 44** Cellar restaurant in Grand-Place that offers tasty food, friendly service and a setting of unrivalled ambience for a modest price.

L'Auberge des Chapeliers *1-3 Rue des Chapeliers* ☎ **02 513 73 38** Belgian specialities in a bistro-style setting near Grand-Place.

Regional Beers

Beer is the traditional drink in Belgium, which has some 400 different beers to choose from. The majority of them are straightforward *pilsener* (lager) beers like **Stella Artois**, **Jupiler** and **Maes**. Alongside them is a vigorous tradition of specialised regional beers. Most of these are from Flanders and Wallonia, but Brussels has a few highly distinctive performers too.

Lambic, a traditional Brussels beer, is made from wheat, malted barley, hops and water. At the point when yeast would normally be added to the mixture to start fermentation, a *lambic* beer gets instead an infusion of a magic ingredient – ordinary air from the Senne valley, which contains particular micro-organisms. When the wort (beer mix) is exposed to them, spontaneous fermentation begins. The beer is matured for one or two years in big kegs called *foudres*, fermenting at its own pace and without the introduction of yeast.

The most popular beers brewed using this method are **gueuze**, **kriek** and **framboise**. To make *gueuze*, two *lambic* beers from different years are mixed and put into Champagne-style bottles in which a second fermentation takes place, brought about by the sugar content of the younger *lambic*. The resulting fizzy beer, served in Champagne glasses, has a characteristic sharp taste. To produce *kriek*, the brewer steeps cherries in *lambic*, and for *framboise* he steeps raspberries, or adds the juice of these fruits during the last stage of fermentation, giving the beer a fresh, fruity tang.

There used to be dozens of breweries in the city making *lambic* beer but now there is only one – the **Cantillon Brewery** in Anderlecht, which has a Gueuze Museum (*see* p.71).

The most important regional beer, indeed Belgium's most popular brew, is **Stella Artois**, made by Interbrew in Leuven. Although considered a premium product in other countries, such as the United States and Britain, Stella's low-fermentation *pilsener* is regarded as an ordinary beer in Belgium, even if it is a popular one.

Le Marmiton *43 Rue des Bouchers* ☎ **02 511 79 10** Fine Belgian food in the atmospheric but occasionally indifferent Îlot Sacré district.

Le Scheltema *7 Rue des Dominicains* ☎ **02 512 20 84** Perennially popular brasserie-restaurant; standard Belgian dishes served to high quality.

St-Catherine–Marché-aux-Poissons

La Truite d'Argent *Quai aux Bois-à-Brûler 23* ☎ **02 219 95 46** Seafood is the speciality of this fine Fish Market restaurant.

La Belle Maraîchère *11 Place St-Catherine* ☎ **02 512 97 59** A good choice from the many seafood restaurants in the area; charming setting.

Saint-Géry

Fin de Siècle *9 Rue des Chartreux* ☎ **02 513 51 23** An atmospheric café-restaurant in a trendy area. A range of simple but tasty dishes.

In 't Spinnekopke *1 Place du Jardin-aux-Fleurs* ☎ **02 511 86 95** Traditional food in a rambling, wood-beamed 17C house.

Porte de Namur

Au Trappiste *7 Avenue de la Toison-d'Or* ☎ **02 511 78 39** Stands out for good quality at reasonable prices in an area where expensive restaurants abound.

Au Vieux Bruxelles *35 Rue Saint-Boniface* ☎ **02 513 01 81** An 1880s brasserie which serves mussels in a wide range of styles.

Ixelles

La Quincaillerie *45 Rue du Page*

The traditional café, À la Mort Subite.

☎ **02 538 25 53** Seafood tops the bill at this stylish restaurant in an old-fashioned former hardware store.

Cafés

L'Amadeus *13 Rue Veydt* ☎ **02 538 34 27** A wine bar (unusual in this country of beer) in the former studio of Rodin.

Café Greenwich *7 Rue des Chartreux* ☎ **02 511 41 67** Enjoy a drink in a beautiful Art Nouveau setting, and play chess just as René Magritte did.

La Fleur en Papier Doré *55 Rue des Aléxiens* ☎ **02 511 16 59** Bohemian haunt in a converted 17C house. The city's Surrealist artists used to meet here.

À la Mort Subite *7 Rue des Montagnes-aux-Herbes Potagères* ☎ **02 513 13 18** The name of this marvellous old café comes from a strong type of beer, and means 'Sudden Death'.

Théâtre Toone VII *6 Impasse Schuddeveld, 21 Petite Rue des Bouchers* ☎ **02 511 71 37** Traditional bar-cum-puppet theatre, where the marionette interpretations of classic stories in several languages, including Brussels dialect, produce a fascinating experience.

De Ultieme Hallucinatie *316 Rue Royale* ☎ **02 217 06 14** Convivial Art Nouveau gem that's a firm favourite with the city's Flemish community.

SHOPPING

Though not as celebrated a shopping destination as Paris, London or Milan – and in Belgium Antwerp is generally rated higher – Brussels nevertheless has no shortage of shopping opportunities. This applies across the price range, which is extending all the time thanks to the increasing number of international visitors and residents with plenty of disposable income. Belgian products worth looking out for as souvenirs include diamonds, lace, crystal, pralines, beer, cheese, Ardennes hams and pâté.

Among prominent shopping streets and districts in the lower city, pedestrianised **Rue Neuve**, which runs from Place de la Monnaie to Place Rogier, together with some adjacent streets, contain popular chain stores, boutiques and department stores. Shopping malls in this area include **City 2** and the **Anspach Center**. **Rue Antoine Dansaert**, facing the Bourse, is the place for bohemian and avant-garde designer fashion.

Shopping galleries abound. In the city centre these include **Galeries Saint-Hubert**, near Grand-Place, a graceful arcade from 1847 with three corridors containing classy shops and cafés. Adjacent **Galerie Agora**

Belgian lace.

goes in for modestly priced, youth-oriented goods, and nearby **Galerie Bortier** is good for antiques and secondhand books.

If you seek the big international names in fashion and luxury goods, head for the upper city, to **Avenue Louise**, and adjacent Boulevard de Waterloo and Avenue de la Toison d'Or at the Place Stéphanie end of the avenue, going as far as Porte de Namur. You'll find the likes of Burberry's, Cartier, Gianni Versace, Gucci, Louis Vuitton, Nina Ricci and Valentino. Belgian designer Olivier Strelli has a shop on Avenue Louise. **Galerie Louise** has some of the city's most expensive shops.

Markets

There's a small **flower market** in Grand-Place daily from 8am until 6pm and a Sunday **bird market** which is open between 9am and 1pm. Nearby in Place d'Espagne, at the top of Rue du Marché-aux-Herbes, a weekend **crafts market** retails minor items of jewellery and other mostly inexpensive pieces.

The most interesting market is the daily **flea market** which takes place between 7am and 2pm in Place du Jeu-de-Balle in the Marolles district. You'll find all kinds of stuff here, including old records, clothes and household goods ranging from junk to pieces that at least verge on being valuable antiques. In a different league is the **antiques market** in Place du Grand Sablon, where the range and quality of goods – silverware, jewellery, chain watches, pottery, paintings and other items – are exceptional and reflected in the prices; it is open on Saturday from 9am until 6pm, and on Sunday from 9am until 2pm.

The colourful **Sunday market** around Gare du Midi, open between 6am and 1pm, is popular with the city's immigrant communities.

ENTERTAINMENT AND NIGHTLIFE

Don't believe anyone who tells you there's nothing to do in Brussels – you can find everything from classical music concerts and opera to drag shows and puppet theatre. The 'What's On' supplement in the English-language weekly magazine *The Bulletin* lists a full programme of events. Still, it's true that dining out and quaffing a locally-brewed beer in a café are 'entertainment' enough for many people.

If you are in Brussels during the summer months, try not to miss the **sound-and-light show** in Grand-Place. Accompanied by a suitably stirring piece of music, lights on the square's venerable façades, in particular those of the Town Hall, go on and off and change colour in a performance that is kitsch, yet well worth experiencing.

Undoubted star of the city's cultural firmament is the sumptuous **Théâtre Royal de la Monnaie** (*Place de la Monnaie* ☎ **02 229 12 11**), home of the **National Opera** and modern dance group **Rosas**, led by choreographer Anna Theresa de Keersmaeker. Classical ballet is rare, unless the **Koninklijk Ballet van Vlaanderen** happens to be visiting from its Antwerp base. The **Palais des Beaux-Arts** (*10 Rue Royale* ☎ **02 507 82 00**), the city's main venue for classical music, is the home of the **Orchestre National de Belgique**. Other important auditoria include **Cirque Royal** (*81 Rue de l'Enseignement* ☎ **02 218 20 15**), which used to be a circus, and now hosts music, opera and ballet, and the **Conservatoire Royal de Musique** (*30 Rue de la Régence* ☎ **02 511 04 27**).

The French and Dutch languages naturally predominate in the city's theatres, though occasionally you can see plays in English. A prominent venue is the **Koninklijke Vlaamse Schouwburg** (*146 Rue de Laeken* ☎ **02 217 69 37**).

To **book tickets** for live shows and performances ☎ **0800 21 221**. You can also book in

Brass band in Grand-Place.

advance from home ☎ **(00 32) 2 501 29 47**.

Phil's Jazz Kitchen Café (*189 Rue Haute*), a relaxed bar, has jazz or other music most nights of the week, and a Wednesday jam session. **L'Archiduc** (*6 Rue Antoine Dansaert*), a chic Art Deco café, puts on Saturday and Sunday jazz concerts, beginning at 5pm. **Le Travers** (*11 Rue Traversière*) remains the favourite haunt of jazz buffs. For those who like their licks more restrained, there's a Sunday jazz brunch at the **Airport Sheraton Hotel** (facing the airport terminal building) between noon and 3pm.

Top international rock and pop groups on European tours perform at **Forest National** (*36 Avenue du Globe* ☎ **02 340 22 11**) and **Ancienne Belgique** (*110 Boulevard Anspach* ☎ **02 548 24 24**).

Films are generally shown in their original language (which usually means English), with French and Dutch subtitles. Multiplexes include **Kinepolis** (*Bruparck* ☎ **0900 35 241**) which has 28 screens, one of which is an IMAX screen, and **UGC De Brouckère** (*38 Place de Brouckère* ☎ **0900 10 440**), with 12 screens. The **Arenberg Galeries** (*26 Galerie de la Reine*) is more likely to show non-English films.

For nightclubs, try the popular transvestite cabaret and dinner show at **Chez Flo** (*25 Rue au Beurre*). The **Show Point** (*14 Place Stéphanie*) features dance moves by scantily clad showgirls.

Le Fuse (*208 Rue Blaes*), is one of the hottest discos in town, with a strong emphasis on techno, and once a month incorporates the women-only Pussy Lounge on Fridays, and men-only La Démence on Sundays. **Le Sparrow** (*16 Rue Duquesnoy*), just off Grand-Place, is a modern, multi-genre disco that attracts a youthful crowd. More sedate swingers might prefer dancing at **Mirano Continental** (*38 Chaussée de Louvain*) or the **Griffin Club** (*Royal Windsor Hotel, 5 Rue Duquesnoy*).

SPORT

Local soccer hotshots are **RSC Anderlecht**, a proud side which generally picks up a Belgian trophy or two then brings top international clubs to Brussels during subsequent European tournaments (held in the Stade Vanden-Stock). The Belgian national team generally plays at the King Baudouin Stadium (Stade Roi Baudouin), otherwise known as the Heysel, near the Atomium.

Horse racing fans will find plenty of action at **Hippodrome de Boitsfort** (*51 Chaussée de la Hulpe*); **Renbaan van Groenendaal** (*4 Sint-Jansberglaan, Hoeilaart*); and **Renbaan van Sterrebeek** (*43 du Roy de Blicquylaan, Sterrebeek*). If you prefer to ride horses yourself, rather than watch other people doing it, the **Bois de la Cambre** (*Centre équestre de la Cambre, 872 Chemin de Waterloo, 1000 Brussels* ☎ **02 375 34 08**) and **Forêt de Soignes** (*Royal Étrier Belge, 19 Champ du Vert Chasseur, 1000 Brussels* ☎ **02 374 28 60**) have good bridle paths and local stables.

There are plenty of tennis courts, squash courts, and health and fitness centres – your hotel will know the nearest ones. There's an Olympic-size swimming pool at the **Centre Sportif de Woluwe-Saint-Pierre** (*2 Avenue Salome*); a good pool at **Poseidon** (*4 Avenue des Vaillants, Woluwe-Saint-Lambert*), which also has an ice-skating rink; and **Océade** water park at Bruparck.

If you want to play golf at one of the five courses around the city, contact the **Fédération Royal Belge de Golf** (*110 Chaussée de la Hulpe* ☎ **02 672 22 22**).

A spot of quiet fishing on the banks of Lake Genval, Rixensart.

THE BASICS

Before You Go

Visitors from the UK and other EU countries entering Belgium should have a full passport (valid for the period in which they will be travelling) or a valid visitor's card for stays of up to 90 days. No visa is required for nationals of EU countries. Nationals of the USA, Canada, Australia and New Zealand need a valid passport and can stay for up to three months without a visa. A visa is required for all other countries outside the EU.
No vaccinations are necessary.

Getting There

By Train: Rail travel is the ideal means of travelling to Brussels from the UK and elsewhere within Europe, for Belgian trains are frequent, fast and punctual. **Eurostar** runs 11 services a day, at roughly two-hourly intervals, between London Waterloo and Brussels Midi (Zuid), taking 2 hours 40 minutes. The difference between first-class and standard accommodation is not great but a meal is included with the first-class fare. Booking a week in advance substantially reduces fares, as does an overnight stay including Saturday night. For bookings and enquiries ☎ **0990 186 186**, or book through your local travel agent or railway station.

For information on train schedules and prices in Belgium, contact Belgian National Railways: Blackfriars Foundary, 156 Blackfriars Road, London SE1 8EN ☎ **(020) 7593 2332**; or in Brussels ☎ **02 555 25 25**.

By Air: Belgium's national airport is at Zaventem, 14km (9 miles) outside Brussels, and is served by most airlines. **Sabena** (Belgian World Airlines) has regular flights from London Heathrow and most other main UK airports. For information contact Sabena:
London: ☎ **020 8780 14 44**; *Brussels*: for general information ☎ **02 723 31 11**; reservations ☎ **02 723 23 23**; flight times ☎ **02 723 23 45**. Trains run every 20 minutes from Zaventem airport to the Gare du Nord, Gare Centrale and Gare du Midi in Brussels. The journey time is approximately 20 minutes and costs around 90BF.

By Sea: There are various options for visitors crossing the English Channel by boat. P&O European Ferries operate between Dover and Calais (approximately 75 minutes), while the overnight P&O North Sea Ferries cross between Hull and Zeebrugge (approximately 14 hours) ☎ **(01482) 37 71 77**. Holyman Sally Ferries sail between Dover and Ostend, with ferries taking about 4 hours while the new catamaran service takes 1 hour 40 minutes ☎ **(01843) 59 55 22**. Hoverspeed Seacat service runs to Ostend, where easy connections can be made by rail to Brussels ☎ **08705 240 241**.

By Car: If you are taking your car either you can use one of the above ferry crossings or a quicker option is the frequent **Le Shuttle** drive-on train service (35 minutes) between Folkestone and Calais through the Channel Tunnel ☎ **0990 35 35 35**. There is a good network of autoroutes connecting the main cities in Belgium. For visitors from the UK, the easiest route is from Ostend, along the A 10 and E 40 (115km/72 miles). From Calais, the drive is further, either going along the E 40 via Ostend (213km/132 miles) or taking the E 42 to Lille, then the A 8 to Brussels (231km/144 miles).

By Coach: Several coach companies run services between London and Brussels. **Eurolines** operate a service (3 times a day in summer, twice a day in winter) from Victoria Station, London, to Brussels Gare du Nord railway station. Using Le Shuttle, this takes around 7 hours. For information ☎ **0990 14 32 19** or **(01582) 40 45 11**.

Cartoon figure near the Comic Strip Museum.

A-Z

Accidents and Breakdowns

Contact the rental firm in the event of an accident or breakdown. Breakdown services are operated by **Touring Secours ☎ (070) 344 777** and **RACB ☎ 287 09 11**. If you have an accident, exchange names, addresses and insurance details but on no account move the vehicle, even if you are causing a hold up, as this may affect your insurance claim. In the event of an accident call the emergency number **☎ 100**. For police **☎ 101**. *See also* **Driving** and **Emergencies**

Accommodation see p.98

Banks

Banks are open Mon-Fri 9am-4pm, though some close for an hour at lunchtime. A passport is required if you are changing money. Automated teller machines (ATMs) can be found in most banks in the city. There is a standard commission for changing travellers' cheques and foreign currency but you should always check the rate of exchange being offered. Generally bureaux de change offer the best rates, followed by banks. Travellers' cheques and cash can also be changed at most hotels, although the exchange rate may not be very favourable. *See also* **Money**

Camping

All official campsites are classified with a star rating according to the facilities they offer. A camp site opened in the city in 1996 at Bruxelles sous les Étoiles, 205 Chaussée de Wavre, 1050 Brussels **☎ 02 653 62 15**. There are numerous others within a reasonable distance of the city. The Belgian Tourist Office has a brochure listing all the campsites in the region.

Car Hire

All the main international car-hire firms and local agencies are represented at the airport and in Brussels itself (especially at the Gare du Midi railway station). Accidents are frequent so you are strongly advised to take out collision damage waiver. If you require a car with automatic transmission you should specify this when booking.

Most companies restrict hire of cars to drivers over 25 and under 70. Drivers must have held a full licence for at least a year. Unless paying by credit card, a substantial cash deposit is required. *See also* **Driving** and **Accidents and Breakdowns**

Climate see p.96

Clothing

The weather can be unpredictable at all times of the year, so you should be prepared for rain, even during the summer months. Spring can be very pleasant, with bright sunny days, but the wind can be chill, as can the evenings, so it is advisable to wear several layers that can be taken off or put on as necessary.

Mini-Europe, Bruparck.

Casual wear is generally acceptable, although smarter clothing will not be out of place at 5-star hotels and more exclusive restaurants. Remember to dress appropriately when visiting churches.

Most clothing measurements are standard throughout Europe but differ from those in the UK and the USA. The following are examples:

Women's sizes

UK	8	10	12	14	16	18
Europe	38	40	42	44	46	48
US	6	8	10	12	14	16

Women's shoes

UK	4.5	5	5.5	6	6.5	7
Europe	38	38	39	39	40	41
US	6	6.5	7	7.5	8	8.5

Men's suits

UK/US	36	38	40	42	44	46
Europe	46	48	50	52	54	56

Men's shirts

UK/US	14	14.5	15	15.5	16	16.5	17
Europe	36	37	38	39/40	41	42	43

Men's shoes

UK	7	7.5	8.5	9.5	10.5	11
Europe	41	42	43	44	45	46
US	8	8.5	9.5	10.5	11.5	12

Consulates and Embassies

Australia Rue Guimard 6, 1040 Brussels ☎ **02 231 0500**
Canada Avenue de Tervuren 2, 1040 Brussels ☎ **02 735 6040**
Republic of Ireland Rue de Luxembourg 19-21, 1040 Brussels ☎ **02 513 6633**
New Zealand Boulevard de Regent 47-48, 1000 Brussels ☎ **02 512 1040**
UK Rue Arlon 85, 1040 Brussels ☎ **02 287 6211**
USA Boulevard du Regent 27, 1000 Brussels ☎ **02 513 3830**

Crime

There is no need to be unduly concerned about crime in Brussels. The city prides itself on the fact that while it is not crime-free, crime is kept firmly under control. It is, however, advisable to take sensible precautions and be on your guard at all times. Pick-pockets and bag-snatchers are at work, as in any European city, so you should remember the following guidelines:

• Carry as little money and as few credit cards as possible, and leave any valuables in the hotel safe.
• Carry wallets and purses in secure pockets inside your outer clothing, and carry handbags across your body or firmly under your arm.
• Never leave the car unlocked and remove items of value.
• If your passport is lost or stolen, report the fact at once to your holiday representative, Consulate or Embassy.

Currency *see* Money

Customs and Taxes

There is no restriction on the amount of Belgian or foreign currency that can be brought into or taken out of the country.

Personal belongings and clothing intended for your own use are not liable to duty.

Hotel and restaurants include VAT and service in their prices. Visitors from non-EU countries who buy an item in Belgium costing more than 7 000BF are entitled to a refund of the VAT (19%), which is included in the price. Ask at the time of purchase for details of how to reclaim this.

Disabled Visitors

In Britain, RADAR, at 12 City Forum, 250 City Road, London EC1V 8AF ☎ **(020) 7250 3222**, publishes factsheets as well as an annual guide to facilities and accommodation overseas, including Belgium.

The booklet *Bâtiments accessible aux handicapés en chaise roulante* lists all public buildings, shops, post offices, banks and so on which are accessible to wheelchair-users, and is available from the Belgian Red Cross. This organisation can also give advice to disabled visitors to Belgium on matters such as the hire of aids and equipment. You should write well in advance to Croix Rouge de Belgique, 98 Chaussée de Vleurgat, 1050 Brussels ☎ **02 645 44 11** Fax 02 640 31 96.

There are special facilities for travellers with disabilities at some Belgian railway stations. Enquire in advance to Belgian National Railways, Premier House, 10 Greycoat Place, London SW1P 1SB ☎ **(020) 7976 00 41**.

Driving

Drivers should carry a full national or international driving licence. If you are taking your own car, you should also take a nationality sticker for the rear of the car, the registration papers and insurance documents, including a green card (no longer compulsory for EU members but strongly recommended).

The headlights need to be adjusted for driving on the right-hand side of the road. You are required by law to carry a red warning triangle and a first-aid kit. You should also have a spare set of light bulbs.

The roads are well maintained and the free motorway network (no tolls) means you can travel from one end of the country to the other in around

Cafés and restaurants line the streets of the Îlot Sacré district.

3 hours. The following speed limits apply:

Motorways 120kph/75mph
Major country roads 90kph/56mph
Built-up areas 50kph/31mph

Speeding tickets are issued on the spot and have to be paid within 48 hours.

Remember to drive on the right-hand side of the road. The wearing of seat belts is compulsory in both front and rear seats, and children under 12 must be seated in the rear. Drinking and driving is severely penalised.

It is not really advisable for visitors to drive in Brussels, and even the attractions in the outlying districts are easily reached by public transport. Most of the city lends itself to exploration on foot, so leave your car at your hotel, if there are parking facilities, or leave it at one of the city car parks. You will need 5 or 20BF coins for the parking meters. *See also* **Accidents and Breakdowns** and **Emergencies**

Electric Current

The voltage in Belgium is usually 220V, using a standard two-pin round continental plug, so visitors should bring adaptors.

Embassies *see* Consulates

Emergencies

Police ☎ **101**. The basic accident emergency/ambulance/fire/rescue number is ☎ **100** (there will always be at least one English-speaking operator on call).

Etiquette

Belgian people are noted for their generous hospitality and the pride that they take as hosts. There are no particular rules of etiquette that are different from those in the UK. Women travelling alone should take the usual precautions.

Health

Belgium has an excellent health service funded by the State, national insurance and private medical insurance. Under the Reciprocal Health Arrangements, visitors from EU countries are entitled to the same standard of treatment in an emergency as Belgian nationals. To qualify, you should carry an E111 form (available from post offices in Britain). This does not cover all medical expenses, and you are advised to take out health insurance to cover your visit. You will be expected to meet the cost of treatment in the first instance and can claim back 75% of the cost with the E111 form.

	French	Dutch
Good morning	Bonjour	Goedemorgen
Good afternoon	Bonjour	Goedenamiddag
Good evening	Bonsoir	Goedenavond
Goodbye	Au revoir	Tot ziens
Please	S'il vous plaît	Alstublieft
Thank you	Merci	Dank u wel
Yes	Oui	Ja
No	Non	Nee
How much?	Combien?	Hoeveel?
Excuse me/sorry	Pardon	Pardon
Do you speak English?	Parlez-vous anglais?	Spreekt u Engels?
How much is it?	Quel est le prix?	Hoeveel?
I want to buy ...	Je voudrais acheter ...	Ik wil graag ...

Hotels hold a list of doctors and dentists. Pharmacists are used to diagnosing minor complaints and will refer you to a doctor if they feel this is necessary.

Language

Brussels is officially bi-lingual, with both French and Dutch spoken. Although German is Belgium's third official language, you will be more likely to hear English than German in Brussels.

The city is mainly French-speaking, so it will probably be the language you will use locally. Don't underestimate the charms of Dutch, though; if you try using a few words when you're in a Flemish environment, you'll probably find your listeners more delighted than French speakers, who take it for granted that visitors can speak French. Above are a few words and phrases in French and Dutch to help you communicate.

Maps

The Michelin Road Map **No 909** Belgium/Luxembourg (1:350 000), which covers the whole country, will help with route-planning and excursions from Brussels. The more detailed Michelin Map **No 213** Bruxelles/Oostende/Liège

(1:200 000) also indicates many tourist attractions en route and **No 3213** (1:150 000) covers an area of 40km (25 miles) around Brussels. The Michelin **City Plan 44 Brussels** provides a detailed street plan of the city, with a street index. The *Michelin Green Guide Brussels* includes full information on all the key sights and attractions in the city, with detailed street plans and background information. The Michelin *Green Guide Belgium and Luxembourg* covers the excursions. The *Michelin Red Guide Benelux* provides details of accommodation and has a list of selected restaurants. The tourist offices also provide street maps of Brussels, together with transport maps.
Michelin on the Net:
www.michelin-travel.com
Our route-planning service covers all of Europe. Options allow you to choose a route and these are updated three times weekly, integrating ongoing road-works, etc. The descriptions include distances and travelling times between towns, selected hotels and restaurants.

Money

The monetary unit of Belgium is the Belgian franc (abbreviated BEF or BF), which comes in 1, 5, 20 and 50 franc coins, and a 50 centime coin (100 centimes = 1 franc). Bank notes are available for 100, 200, 500, 1 000, 2 000 and 10 000BF. Credit cards are widely accepted – most commonly Visa, American Express, Diners Club and Eurocard. Eurocheques endorsed with a Eurocheque card can be used for sums up to 7 000BF.

On 1 January 1999, the **euro** became the offical common currency between 11 countries, including Belgium. Bank notes and coins will be introduced in all 11 countries on 1 January 2002. From then on, it will no longer be necessary to change money when travelling in the euro zone countries.

Perhaps the safest way to carry large amounts of money is in travellers' cheques, which are widely accepted. Lost or stolen travellers' cheques and credit cards should be reported immediately to the issuing company, with a list of numbers; the police should also be informed.

Bureaux de change desks are found at the airport and banks. Exchange rates vary, so it pays to shop around. You are advised not to pay hotel bills in foreign currency or with travellers' cheques since the

hotel's exchange rate is likely to be higher than that of the bureaux de change.
See also **Banks**

Newspapers

British and foreign newspapers and magazines can be bought in the main cities at newsagents and kiosks, usually the same day. The *International Herald Tribune* and British dailies such as the *Financial Times, Daily Telegraph* and *The Times* are readily available.

The local daily papers are useful for tourists as they include leisure sections, transport timetables, and other relevant practical information.

Opening Hours

Shops: Traditional shop opening hours are 9am-6pm, Mon-Sat. Small shops, bakeries and news-stands may open as early as 7.30/8am. Shops are closed on Sundays but patisseries and other specialist food shops may open in the morning. Outside the city, shops may close at noon for an hour or so, in which case they will usually remain open until 7 or 8pm.

Chemists: These are generally open 8.30am-5.30/6.30pm, Mon-Fri, and Saturday mornings. Emergency cover is provided at night, on Sundays and bank holidays. Lists of chemists which are open late or on Sundays can be found outside each pharmacy.

Museums: As a general rule, the large public museums and galleries are open 10am-5pm every day except Mondays. Other museums may be open on Mondays but are closed on another day of the week. The tourist offices have full details of the opening hours for all the main attractions. *See also* **Banks** and **Post Offices**

Police

If you need assistance, you should approach the Police/*Politie*, who wear dark blue uniforms and usually speak English. A separate

Great Hunt mosaic of Apamea, Musée du Cinquantenaire.

national force, the Gendarmerie/*Rijkswacht*, deals with major crime and polices the motorways; the uniform is a lighter blue, with red trouser stripes. ☎ **101** for the police.

Post Offices
Post offices are usually open 9am-5pm, Mon-Fri, with smaller branches closing at noon for an hour or two. Some larger ones open on Saturday mornings, and the one on the first floor of the Centre Monnaie (Place de la Monnaie) is open on Saturdays 9am-3pm. Stamps are also sold in post offices, by newsagents, and in many hotels.

Public Holidays
New Year's Day: 1 January
Easter Monday: variable
Labour Day: 1 May
Ascension Day:
(sixth Thursday after Easter)
Whit Monday: (seventh Monday after Easter)
National/Independence Day: 21 July
Assumption Day: 15 August
All Saints' Day: 1 November
Armistice Day: 11 November
Christmas Day: 25 December

Public offices and institutions are also closed on 15 November (Dynasty Day) and 26 December (Boxing Day).

Religion
Belgium is predominantly a

Notre Temps *fresco, by Roger Somville, Hankar metro station.*

Roman Catholic country and mass is celebrated in most churches every Sunday. For details of services in other languages, or of churches of other denominations, ask at the local tourist board or at your hotel.

Smoking

No smoking signs are easily identifiable and should be obeyed at all times, but no-smoking sections in restaurants and bars are rare. Smoking sections are allocated on all trains, but smoking is not allowed on other forms of public transport.

Telephones

Public telephones take 5BF, 20BF and 50BF coins, and most will also take phone cards or telecards. Telecards can be bought at tobacconists, newsagents, post offices and public transport ticket offices, for either 200BF or 1000BF. Phones accepting the card can be identified by a telecard sign. The Belgacom office at 17 Boulevard de l'Impératrice, near the central railway station, is open daily, 8am-8pm.

As in most countries, telephone calls made from hotels may be more straightforward and convenient, but they are much more expensive.

Cheap rates apply 6.30pm-8am Mon-Sat, and all day Sunday.

For local directory enquiries ☎ **1207** (Dutch), **1307** (French).

For international operator and international directory enquiries ☎ **1204** (Dutch), **1304** (French).

Country codes are as follows:
Australia ☎ **00 61**
Canada ☎ **00 1**
Ireland ☎ **00 353**
New Zealand ☎ **00 64**
UK ☎ **00 44**
USA ☎ **00 1**

To call the United Kingdom from Belgium, dial **00 44** followed by the local dialling code and the subscriber number. The country code for Belgium is ☎ **00 32**. All numbers in Brussels start with **02**. To call Brussels from abroad, delete the 0 in the city code (dial **00 32 2** plus the subscriber number).

Time Difference

Belgium is on Central European Standard Time, one hour ahead of Greenwich Mean Time (GMT) in winter and two hours ahead in summer. For most of the year, Brussels is therefore one hour ahead of the time in the United Kingdom, five hours ahead of US Eastern Standard, and 14 hours behind Australia (Sydney).

Tipping

In restaurants, a 16% service charge is usually included in the bill (along with 19% VAT), so you are not expected to tip unless you are exceptionally pleased with the service. You may wish to leave any small change for table service at a bar or café but this is not essential.

Hotels also include a service charge in the bill so there is no need to tip porters or room service.

It is usual to give a cinema usher a small tip of around 20BF; in public lavatories there is usually a bowl for coins if you wish to leave a gratuity (10BF).

Tourist Information Offices

It is well worth contacting the **Belgian Tourist Office** before you go. The international branches cover all the regions and can provide you with basic up-to-date information as well as very useful maps and plans. In London, the address of Tourism Flanders-Brussels is 31 Pepper Street, E14 9RW ☎ **0891 88 77 99** Fax (020) 7458 00 45.

In Brussels the **TIB (Office de Tourisme et d'Information de Bruxelles)** at City Hall, Grand-Place, 1000 Brussels ☎ **02 513 89 40** Fax 02 514 45 38, is outstandingly efficient. Whether you are planning a short or long stay, a visit to the local office is strongly recommended at the first opportunity. They will provide information on tours and current entertainments, hotel and restaurant guides, well-produced glossy brochures with maps, and a 'Tourist Passeport' that entitles you to reductions and includes two one-day travel passes on public transport (300BF).

The **OPT (Belgian Tourist Office)**, 63 Rue du Marché-aux-Herbes, 1000 Brussels ☎ **02 504 03 90** Fax 02 504 02 70 also provides information about Brussels.

Tours

A number of specialist firms offer a variety of tours of the city. Check first at the **TIB** tourist office, in Grand-Place ☎ **02 513 89 40**, both for details of their own guided tours during the summer and for other companies. **Arcadia** (53 Rue du Métal, 1060 Brussels ☎ **02 534 38 19**) and **Itinéraires** (157 Rue Hôtel des Monnaies, 1060 Brussels ☎ **02 539 04 34)** both organise thematic tours. **Brussels by Water** (2 bis, Quai des Péniches, 1020 Brussels ☎ **02 203 64 06**) offer boat trips. **De Boeck's Sightseeing-tours** (8 Rue de la Colline,

1000 Brussels ☎ **02 513 77 44**) tour the city by coach, and also offer a 'hop-on-hop-off' service, making 11 stops at key sights (tickets valid for 24hrs, adults 490BF, children 300BF). A bird's-eye view from a helicopter is provided by **Helitour** (40 Ave Joseph Wybran, 1070 Brussels ☎ **02 361 21 21**). The more energetic can explore the city by bike with **Pro vélo** (13-15 Rue de Londres, 1050 Brussels ☎ **02 502 73 55**; summer only). **Le Fonderie** (27 Rue Ransfort, 1080 Brussels ☎ **02 410 99 50**) specialises in the city's industrial heritage, with walking, coach and boat tours, including a harbour tour. **ARAU** (55 Bvd A Max, 1000 Brussels ☎ **02 219 33 45**) offer tours specialising in architectural themes, such as Art Nouveau and Art Deco. **Chatterbus** (12 Rue des Thuyas, 1179 Brussels ☎ **02 673 18 35**) offer an original way to discover the city on various thematic tours, by coach or on foot, with enthusiastic guides.

Transport

The city has a very efficient system of public transport, and visitors arriving by car should leave their car in one of the many car parks, or in the hotel car park. Driving in Brussels, as in most cities, is not easy, although the underpasses along the inner ring road make arriving or travelling

Ommegang parade.

around the city to make excursions much easier.

The STIB (Société des Transports Intercommunaux de Bruxelles) provides a network of tram, bus and metro services which operate in the city and extend to the towns within Greater Brussels. For information on routes and timetables ☎ **02 515 20 00** (Mon-Fri 8am-7pm, Sat 8am-4pm). Maps and a useful brochure explaining how to use the system are available from main stations and the TIB tourist office.

Tickets, which can be used on buses, trams and the metro, can be bought from ticket offices at the stations, from automatic machines in some stations, on buses and trams (have the exact money ready) or from selected commercial agents. A **single ticket** enables you to make a single journey on the bus, tram and metro network (valid for one hour; you can make a connection within the journey, in which case the ticket is valid for up to two hours). The **10-journey ticket** is valid on urban routes only. The **one-day ticket** allows unlimited journeys throughout the entire network during the day. You must validate your ticket at the barrier in metro stations and on boarding buses and trams.

Metro: The underground system operates from 5.30am to half past midnight. The main line crosses the city from east to west and has four termini (Heysel, H Debroux, Stockel and Bizet). A second line, the inner ring, cuts across the main line. Entrances to the underground stations are indicated by a sign with a large white 'M' on a blue background.

Trams: The bright yellow trams are a key feature of the city scenery. There are 15 routes, some of which (called the *prémétro*) are channelled underground in tunnels to avoid the worst of the traffic congestion. Tram no 94 is used for sightseeing trips, running from Jette to Boitsfort, with a commentary at each stop.

Buses: Bus routes cover most of the city and the urban areas, connecting with the tram and metro system.

Taxis: These can be hailed in the street or called by telephone:
Taxis verts ☎ **02 349 49 49**;
Taxis orange ☎ **02 349 43 43**.

TV and Radio

BBC long-wave and world services can easily be picked up, and cable TV channels are available at many hotels.

INDEX